# THE STORY OF MY FATHER

# THE STORY OF MY FATHER

## Sue Miller

CHIVERS

| British Library Cataloguing in Publication Data available |
| --- |

This Large Print edition published by BBC Audiobooks Ltd, Bath, 2005.
Published by arrangement with Bloomsbury Publishing Plc

U.K. Hardcover ISBN 1 4056 3382 4
U.K. Softcover   ISBN 1 4056 3383 2

500 850 882

Printed and bound in Great Britain by
Antony Rowe Ltd., Chippenham, Wiltshire

The names of some characters and places in this memoir have been changed to protect anonymity.

# CHAPTER ONE

Some quality in my father's voice always changed when he spoke of my uncles—the one who'd been incarcerated in a federal prison in the Second World War, and the one who'd given a year of his life at that time to alternate service. I don't remember now how or even whether my father explained their choices to me, or how I came to know what those choices were; but long before I understood any of that, I understood by the shift in my father's voice how much he admired them. I understood that he believed they'd done the right thing, the hard thing.

They were conscientious objectors, my uncles, in a war that was seen as 'good' and 'just'—though they made their stand even before America entered that war, when they were required to register for the draft in 1940, the first peacetime draft in the nation's history. Both of my uncles felt that even in a just war—perhaps especially in a just war—men should follow their conscience. Like my father, both were radical Christians. They believed that the Jesus who conceived of human life as having the potential for moral goodness was speaking of a necessary *action* to be taken when he called on his followers to love their enemies, to pray for those who persecuted them, to turn

1

the other cheek to those who struck them.

And so my uncles acted. One of them refused to acknowledge that the state might have the right to command him to kill another human being and didn't register at all; he was the one who went to jail. The other registered but asked to be exempted from that command on religious grounds and was given alternative service.

For years I didn't think to question my father about his own choices during World War Two. I suppose I assumed, on those rare occasions when it might have occurred to me to think about it at all, that he had escaped the issue somehow because of having children— my older brother was born in August of 1941. I'm not sure when I learned he'd taken the exemption available to him as an ordained minister, or whether that too was just an assumption, accurate in this case. At any rate, it is what I finally assumed. And then further assumed that the tone of awe and admiration that rose in his voice for my uncles, and for his other pacifist friends who did what my uncles did, rose because he admired their greater courage, their greater conviction than his own. Certainly he never said anything that would have led me to think anything else.

After his death, though, I was sorting through the few papers he'd left behind and I came upon a letter that called up for question all of my assumptions. It was addressed to my

2

father in October of 1940, and it was from another young man, also a minister, someone who must have believed—as, it became clear, my father had too—that when Christ spoke of loving your enemies, he was asking for something rather specific from you.

The letter said:

> Dear Mr. Nichols: It was a great joy to learn that I am not the only person in this part of the country who has decided that there can be absolutely no compromise with conscription. Notice of your refusal to register and a copy of your statement to the registration board reached me by way of a clipping from the *Dispatch* sent by my parents in St. Paul.

The young man went on to ask about my father's family's attitude toward his position, to speak of the support he had from *his* family, to inquire about what the repercussions had been from my father's employer, and ended:

> More strength to you in your stand. Sincerely yours, Rev. Winslow Wilson.

I was stunned, reading this. Everything I'd understood about my father's behavior at that time had been simply wrong. He had *refused*, my father! He had, in fact, taken the most extreme course possible in resisting and because of this had become, momentarily, a public person, written up in the St. Paul *Dispatch.* My father, modest, shy as he was, had made a difficult, unpopular, public stand.

And suddenly it seemed utterly right to me that resistance had been his wish, his intention. It made a kind of emotional sense that caused me to feel, instantly, how little sense my earlier more or less unframed assumptions had made. *Of course!* I thought. And with that thought it was as though my father stepped forward to meet me as he had been in 1940: twenty-five years old, newly married, teaching literature and history and religion at his first real job, as an assistant professor at Macalester College in St. Paul, Minnesota. That stage of his life—and he in it—had always been indistinct to me, as the lives of parents before their children exist always are to those children; but now, holding this letter in my hands, I remembered anew and vividly the numerous photographs in our family albums of him then—a slender young man, intense-looking and handsome, with a shock of dark hair swept back from his high forehead. A radical young man, it would seem. More radical in many ways than my own son was now. A young man ready, perhaps even eager, to embrace the fate his powerful beliefs were calling him to. Sitting there, I felt a rush of love and pity for him in his youth, in his passionate convictions—really, the same feeling I often had for my son when he argued

4

*his* heartfelt positions. Abruptly, they seemed alike to me and equally dear: my father, my son. I felt as though my father had been waiting for this moment to be born to me as the young man he'd been, so touchingly willing to bear witness to his conscience; and the surprise of this new sense of him, this birth, was a gift to me, a sudden balm in those days of my most intense grief.

But what had called him back? What made him turn away from his choice?—which would have been hard, of course, but satisfying too, in the way that acting on our deepest feelings and commitments is always satisfying. What made him take the easier path, the one that kept him safe, home, out of prison—the exemption—but the path that also denied him the satisfaction of acting on his beliefs, that pride of bearing witness?

He'd kept another letter in the envelope with the one from the young Reverend Wilson, and this one I can't quote from; it angered me so much that I threw it away after reading it. It was written a few months after Winslow Wilson's, and it was from my grandfather, my mother's father. It counseled my father against taking the path that beckoned him. As part of its argument, it pointed to my mother's pregnancy—which she must just have discovered—and it suggested, terribly delicately, a kind of vulnerability, perhaps even a slight . . . instability . . . on her part, to which

5

my father would be abandoning her and their child if he were imprisoned. Of course, the letter said, if my father truly felt this was the right thing to do, to ask my mother to manage this difficult situation, he and my grandmother (they lived nearby; he was the pastor of a large and prominent Minneapolis church) would do all they could to provide the support she would need in my father's absence.

There was more. My grandfather called up the contract my father would be breaking with the college, the responsibilities he'd undertaken there that he would be abandoning; but again he affirmed his support, 'of course,' if my father felt this was the right thing to do.

For fifty years my father had kept these two letters together, the one that embraced him in his decision and confirmed his choice to make his life a kind of witness to his faith and beliefs, and the other, which cautioned against it. And during all those years he'd spoken not a word of regret, of bitterness or sorrow, for the choice he'd made in the end. He'd never even made an accounting of that choice in my presence—as if in making his decision he'd lost forever the right to speak of the beliefs he hadn't acted on.

I was sitting in my own sunny living room in Boston when I read these letters. I stayed there for a while, staring out at the red-brick church across the street, thinking about this

6

new sense of my father and welcoming it. And then I remembered, I realized, that I in fact did have a written explanation he'd made of himself and of his choice.

I went up to my study and scrambled through my files of family papers until I found it. It was a homily my father had given at my older brother's wedding. This is it, in its entirety:

There is a certain similarity between marriage and the Christian religion, which is suggested by the text in our gospel reading: 'Ye have not chosen me, but I have chosen you.'

The dominant note at the beginning of marriage is the joy of mutual possessing, of a 'choosing' triumphantly accomplished. And this is as it should be.

So in religion there is at the beginning often a searching and a choosing, an affirming of that good which one may serve with conviction. And this too is as it should be. But in time we see more. We become aware that our seeking and our choosing is not so self-determined as we had thought, but our response to a Seeker who had already found us. We come to understand that text: 'Ye have not chosen me, but I have chosen you.'

So with marriage we understand more in time. Deeper than the joy of a

7

'choosing' triumphantly fulfilled is the awareness of a need to be met, of a claim acknowledged. Few things are as potent to give meaning to life as the sense of answering a need and fulfilling a responsibility which no one else can meet.

It is wonderful indeed that we can choose and achieve our choice, but still more wonderful that we are chosen.

Reading the homily in this new context made it more moving to me than it had been the first times I'd read it. And like the revelation that my father would have chosen to resist conscription, it seemed suddenly *right* to me, more deeply right than before. It made me understand him. My father, a young impassioned man, had chosen twice, and twice he'd chosen in joy and triumph—his faith and my mother. And then it turned out that each of those two choices presented the 'claim' to be 'acknowledged' he spoke of in the homily. Further, it turned out that those claims, as construed by my grandfather and—I must assume—as accepted in that construction by my father, conflicted. My father had to find a way to reconcile them or to decide which claim took precedence. In the event, he honored the personal claim, the smaller, more private one, and never spoke of the decision again.

*     *     *

My older brother's wedding, for which the homily was written, took place in 1968. Sixteen years later, when I was to be married for the second time, I asked my father to preside as minister at the ceremony; and, having checked with my brother and sister-in-law first, I asked him to read the same homily he'd read at their wedding, which I'd found so moving even without yet understanding its fullest implications in my father's life.

My father said yes. But when the moment came for that part of the service, something seemed to go wrong in him. He held the paper in front of him, but he didn't seem to be able to read it. I tried to indicate to him that it was all right—I leaned forward, I think I touched his arm. After a moment, his voice shaking, he spoke a few improvised words in place of the homily and then pronounced his blessing on us.

## CHAPTER TWO

On a June morning in 1986, I was sleeping late in the bright sunshine pouring into my bedroom. This gift for sleep has left me in the seventeen years or so since these events took place, but on that day I'd been enjoying it—

rising up to consciousness, then diving down again for a little while—when I heard the door to the bedroom open. Someone came in. There was a touch on my shoulder and I opened my eyes. My husband was bending over me. His lower face was covered in shaving foam and I was suddenly engulfed in that lathery scent. There were one or two broad dark stripes in the white on his cheek, marking the path of the razor where he'd started to shave and had been interrupted. He looked strange—partly on that account, of course, but partly because there was fear in his face.

He was speaking to me in a deliberately controlled voice, slowly and carefully, but what he was saying made no sense. It was about my father. The police and my father. The police had him. My father. He was somewhere in western Massachusetts. The police were on the phone; they wanted to talk to me.

I was almost instantly up, grabbing for clothing, incoherently asking questions—*What do you mean? what police? western Massachusetts?* I thundered down the stairs to the kitchen, where the only phone was; we had none upstairs because Ben, my son, was seventeen then, and his friends could be counted on, several times a week, to call him after eleven, after twelve—long past the time my husband and I went to bed, in any case. The receiver dangled on the cord from its wall base, almost touching the floor. I picked it up

10

and said hello, said my name, and then stood there, staring out at the start of this beautiful sunny day, trying to make some sense of what the man's voice on the other end of the line was talking about.

What I remember most clearly now is that he said the person they had in custody, James Nichols—they'd picked him up between three and four in the morning in semirural territory when he'd knocked on someone's door, announcing he was lost—'claimed' to be my father.

I was indignant. Of course he was my father. James Nichols? He *was* my father. He *said* so, didn't he? What was their problem?

I didn't know then any of the other claims he'd made: that he'd encountered a number of small strange people in his night-time wandering, that he'd been driving a van, which seemed to have utterly disappeared (they'd scanned the area for it, to no avail). In that context, probably other things he told them— that he was a retired professor from Princeton Theological Seminary, for instance—seemed unlikely too.

But for now it was the word itself, *claimed*, that struck me, in its distrust and dismissal of my father's perspective. It was a word I would come to hear more and more often as Dad descended into illness: well, he claimed he did this; he claimed he saw that; he claimed he thought it was *his* room. But here, this first time with a stranger, it was startling and offensive.

I asked to speak with him. The officer wouldn't let me. He wanted me to come out there. They would release him to me once I arrived.

He wanted to know how long I'd be. I didn't know. Where were they exactly? He gave me general directions and I made a guess.

I got off the phone, and now it was my husband's turn to ask the futile questions. Together, though, as I quickly got ready to go—brushing my teeth, drinking coffee, washing my face—we constructed a story that made a kind of sense.

Under pressure from us, his children, my father had recently agreed to sell his house in New Jersey; we thought he was too isolated there since my mother's death six years earlier. My sister and I had helped him divide up his possessions. Some were shipped ahead to Denver, to an apartment near her where he was going to live for a few years. Some were given away—to the four of us, if we laid claim to them, or to the Salvation Army. Some I had hauled to his summerhouse in New Hampshire in a big rental truck. But there were the last few items left for him to live with until the closing, and he'd told me recently on the phone that he was going to rent a small van and take them up to New Hampshire himself.

What my husband and I concluded now was

12

that it must have been on the way up to or back from this chore that he'd gotten lost in western Massachusetts and somehow seemed confused enough to warrant a kind of detention, if not arrest.

It takes more than two hours to get from Boston to the other end of the state, plenty of time for me to imagine multiple variations on this story, other plot lines that might have led to this outcome. But what I couldn't do for the entire length of the trip was to imagine my father at the center of the drama. That remained a mystery to me: what the actor had felt, what he could have been thinking as he acted. What on earth he was *up* to.

My father was a small man, trim and neat. He had a gentle, nearly apologetic voice. He cleared his throat often, a tic and also a response to chronic dryness. He often had trouble being forceful or direct. I couldn't imagine him—so modest, so self-effacing as to be almost comical sometimes, so much wishing *not* to be trouble for anyone—doing what the police described: stumbling around the countryside trying to wake someone, ringing doorbells in the middle of the night. *Bothering people.* Not my father.

*     *     *

I was appalled when I first saw him, through the glass pane of a door the police pointed me

13

to. He was sitting up, alone in a kind of waiting room set with several chairs. He appeared to be sleeping. When I came into the room, his eyes opened. He saw me with a kind of relief, but with none of the deep recognition that lights a face.

He looked terrible. He was unshaven. He was wearing old clothes, worn and wrinkled and faded. He had on a particularly unfortunate hat he was fond of, a canvas hat he often wore when he went fishing. It was misshapen and stained. He looked like a vagrant—though later it occurred to me that in those same clothes, even wearing that same hat, he had often looked quite different: an outdoorsman ready to pull on waterproof boots and go fishing; a mycologist off to go collecting; a hiker ready to face Mount Adams, Mount Jefferson. So it wasn't the clothes so much, I think, that startled me. It was the vacancy of his face, the look of nonrecognition—not so much of me as of the world—that made him seem homeless, *lost*, in some profound and permanent sense. That revised the meaning of the clothes. That said, 'I belong nowhere, to no one.'

His responses were without depth too. He did apologize for the inconvenience to me, but casually, as though I'd had to drive a few blocks out of the way for him. 'Sorry you had to come get me.' That was it.

He was tired, I told myself. Exhausted.

The police gave me his wallet and the few other possessions they'd taken from him. They still hadn't found the van, they said, and they expressed doubt, in front of him and speaking of him in the third person, that there was such a vehicle. I fell in with this rude behavior, to my shame. With Dad standing right next to me, I said, 'Well, he lives in New Jersey. He must have gotten to western Mass somehow.'

The policeman shrugged. He was a nice man, really. He had told me, before I saw Dad, that the people he'd waked in the night had been frightened of him, he seemed so agitated. He'd told me Dad had been 'seeing things.' Now we agreed that they'd call me when they found the van, and Dad and I drove off.

He was silent in the car, looking diminished and exhausted. We stopped for breakfast, and he ate ravenously. I asked him when he'd eaten last and he couldn't remember. I began to ask him more questions, over breakfast and then again in the car, trying to piece together his itinerary and its timing. It was difficult to figure out. He didn't know exactly when he'd left New Jersey for New Hampshire or what roads he'd taken. He didn't think he'd slept in New Hampshire or eaten. He'd unloaded the furniture by himself (he didn't want to bother anyone else) and then he'd started back down. When? What time? Day or night? He didn't know. Somehow, though, in the night—or was it night? he just didn't know—he'd taken a

15

wrong turn.

By now I realized he was talking about at least twenty hours without sleep and perhaps without food—probably more. I'd been in the house in New Hampshire only a few weeks earlier, unloading the bulk of the furniture from New Jersey. I thought of the way it had felt, cavernous and chilly: the empty unplugged refrigerator, the pervasive smell of the previous owner's cats, the mouse turds everywhere. It was awful to think of him alone there, tired and hungry.

And now he was saying something about the way the stop signs had turned into people in the night. People. Disguised as stop signs. As he talked, describing this, there was suddenly more animation in his face than he'd shown since I first saw him. Delight, really—at how they'd spoken to him in the night. Little people.

'You mean the tops of the stop signs looked like heads to you?' I was already revising his tale, trying to make it something I could imagine too. And I *could*, I could understand this, that you might be charmed by the sudden notion of octagonal fat heads perched on skinny bodies if they loomed up at you on a dark road.

He seemed amused, even a little contemptuous of the flatness of my imagination. 'No, they were people. They had bodies—arms and legs.'

16

I drove for a while, stunned. What was happening to Dad? 'And they spoke to you,' I said at last.

He smiled. 'Yes.'

I stopped asking questions. I couldn't bear to hear the answers. Clearly the police hadn't misrepresented anything: Dad was exactly the confused, disoriented person they had said he was. We drove on in silence, and in a little while he fell asleep. That's what he needs, I thought. Sleep. Food. It was exhaustion, probably some chemical imbalance resulting from his hunger and fatigue, that was making him hallucinatory. As I drove, I looked over at him from time to time, slumped open-mouthed against the car's window, his hat riding the back of his head. I felt very distant from him, even angry at him—for his otherness, for what seemed his unconsciousness of the strangeness of what he was going through and what he'd done. I wanted him restored to himself. I wanted my father back. This old geezer made me mad.

At home, I fixed him another snack and then made up a bed for him in Ben's room. He was happy to take a nap. While he slept—and he slept for some hours—I tried to figure out what to do.

In the short run, the practical complication for me was that my husband and I were leaving for France for a two-month stay in less than a week. Dad obviously would need attention and

17

care for a while, but I couldn't go back to New Jersey and stay with him. On the other hand, I couldn't possibly send him to New Jersey by himself, not as he was, to deal with the final clearing out and cleaning of the house, with his dog, who must be waiting for him with friends or in a kennel, with the van, missing somewhere in the countryside.

I'm a list maker—I live by them—and I already had a long list of errands to do to get ready to go away. Now at the top of that list would have to be my father, and directly under him, ahead of my own concerns, there would be *his* list of things to do. I felt overwhelmed. I couldn't manage this alone. Someone else, one of my siblings, would have to come to help out. Or Dad would have to go to one of them. Or I would have to postpone my going to France; my husband could go on alone, and I'd join him when I could.

My husband came home and I told him some of what seemed to be happening with my father. We discussed the various possibilities. He was open to any of them but of course preferred one that let me go with him. We'd see, we kept saying. We'd see how he was when he woke up. We'd play it by ear.

\*　　　\*　　　\*

Ben's room, where my father was sleeping, was in the basement of the house, a big finished

18

space at the back, with a low ceiling. To get from it to the stairs up to the first floor, you had to pass through the unfinished front part of the basement, dominated by the old, cast-iron coal furnace, converted to gas, and its tentacled ducts; and home to the washer and dryer, the cast-off furniture, the junk of our twelve years in the house—we had no attic. Late in the afternoon, I heard odd noises in that part of the basement. I called down, and after a moment Dad appeared in the dim light at the bottom of the stairs, his lifted face smiling. He looked more like himself, I thought, in that he seemed *present*; he seemed to see me with pleasure.

'Come on up,' I said. 'Have some coffee or a drink or whatever.'

Our conversation as I fixed coffee was easy. How he'd slept. How he might have gotten lost. Where he thought the van might be. He and my husband, who hadn't seen each other for a while, chatted about events and concerns in their lives. He seemed all right; he seemed fine. I began to relax. We went to sit in the living room with our cups. And then Dad said, 'You know, the little children in the basement wouldn't say a word when I spoke to them. They wouldn't answer me.' He seemed puzzled by this, perhaps a little hurt.

I was quiet for a moment. I met my husband's eye. I felt as though I'd been hit. 'What little children do you mean?' I asked, in

19

what I hoped was only a mildly curious tone.

'Just now, downstairs. Ben and some friends.' He looked momentarily confused. 'Or maybe Ben wasn't there. But they wouldn't answer me when I spoke to them. They just moved away.'

After a moment I said, 'Ben?'

'Well, I'm not sure about Ben. Maybe just some other little children.'

'Dad, Ben is seventeen now. And his friends are big too. There aren't any little children around anymore.'

He didn't look at me. We sat still for a few moments. I drank some of my coffee. My husband started to speak to him gently, said he really didn't think—

'There!' Dad said. 'There goes one!' There was a kind of triumph in his voice.

'Where?' I said.

'There.' He pointed.

I got up. I crossed the room and swung myself around in the area he'd indicated. Our living room was a big open space—I'd torn down all the interior walls on the ground floor when I first bought the house. There were no nooks or hiding places. Just air. And me, standing in it. 'There's no one here, Dad,' I said.

He looked genuinely puzzled. 'He must have gone downstairs,' my father said.

So, after a moment, I suggested we go downstairs too—go downstairs and find the

20

kids.

We descended and stood in the cluttered space. There was a single bare bulb suspended from the ceiling whose light fell wanly over the abandoned junk. 'Where were they, Dad?' I asked him.

He crossed in front of the furnace and began to look among the boxes and cast-offs, pushing things back and forth, perplexed.

'There's nobody here now,' I said.

'No,' he agreed. 'Nobody.' He seemed suddenly tired again. Defeated. He didn't look at me.

After a few moments we went upstairs, silently. We sat down in the living room. Finally I said, 'Dad, I don't think there were any little children down there, even earlier. There aren't little children in and out of this house anymore. There would be no reason for there to be kids in here that I didn't know about. No way for them to get in, even. And we didn't hear them or see them leave.'

He nodded. 'No,' he said.

I tried to speak more lightly. 'God knows, I wish we did still have little children roaming around, but we don't. They just weren't there, Dad.'

After another long pause, he said, 'So I guess I was seeing things.'

'I think you were,' I said. 'Look, you hadn't eaten or slept in a couple of days. That does things to you. Chemically. I think you're

21

exhausted and drained and, yes, that you were seeing things.'

We sat in silence for a while. Finally he smiled ruefully and said, 'Doggone, I never thought I'd lose my *mind.*'

There was an unspoken clause implicit at the start of this sentence—*I've tried to think of all the ways I might get old, but*—and I heard it at least as clearly as I heard the part he spoke. I understood, abruptly, that he had wondered how they would come to him, old age and death, and now he was even a little bemused that they should take this unexpected form as they approached.

I was startled at the time to realize this— that he had thought about it. But now that he is dead, and several others of his generation and the one before it in my family are dead also, it's my turn to think of it—of death—and I do. I wonder how it will come to me. Unlike Dad, though—but largely because of him—I think often of the possibility that I may lose my mind. And when I do, I remember this moment; when my father seemed to be getting the news about his fate, about how it would be for him; when he took it in and accepted it and was, somehow, *interested* in it, all at the same time, before my eyes. It was a moment as characteristic of him as any I can think of in his life, and as brave. Noble, really, I've come to feel.

At the time, though, I didn't think of it this

way. I didn't want to think of it at all. I didn't want to see what he saw, I didn't want to accept the larger meaning of the moment. I began to make excuses again to him—for him—the same excuses I'd been making to myself all day about his behavior. And to my relief, he seemed to accept them. He seemed comforted.

This may just have been a kind of politeness on his part. He saw my distress, after all, and he may simply have been responding to it. Perhaps he knew how much I needed him to agree with me, and so he did. He agreed with me. To be kind. So I wouldn't dwell on it. So I wouldn't be troubled.

I don't know.

At any rate, we moved ahead. My son came home, full of adolescent energy and delighted by the surprise arrival of his grandfather. We had dinner, we talked as though this were an ordinary visit. We touched on some of the problems awaiting us; Dad mentioned his need to get back for the dog, I mentioned finding the van. My husband said he'd dig up some toiletries for Dad, who hadn't shaved or brushed his teeth in a while. Basically, though, we visited. Later in the evening, after Dad had gone to bed, my husband and I again talked about what we should do. In the end, I decided to call my sister to ask for her help.

*     *     *

23

Of course there had been signs earlier. There was the slow weakening of what we might have called his *will* after my mother's death six years before. A lack of direction. But other things too. The time I'd gone to New Jersey for a visit and he clearly had no memory that we'd arranged it—though he was, as always, gracious in his expression of pleasure at seeing me. The time he delivered a five-minute sermon in the church in his summer town when he should have gone on for fifteen or twenty minutes—a sermon that had a kind of eloquence, sentence by sentence, but made almost no sense as a whole and then was over so much too soon. There was a palpable shock in the congregation when it ended; after the service, one kind old lady broke the spell by leaning over to me and saying, 'That's how we like 'em: short and sweet.' A little while after that, an old friend of his asked me for the first time a question I would hear over and over as Dad got sick, 'What do you think is wrong with your father?'

There were problems in class, the first he'd ever had. There were his own reports to me of difficulties with his work. There was his arriving at his youngest sister's house, forty-five minutes away from his own, and telling her he'd had a period of blankness on the road when he couldn't think where he was or where he was supposed to be going. She called me, wondering if I had any idea what was wrong with him. It was on account of all this, after all, that we had urged him to sell the house in New Jersey, where he was so isolated once he retired, and move to Denver to be near my sister.

But Dad was by no means so hapless as this makes him sound. He had functioned on his own after Mother's death, and for the first years he managed it rather well. Whenever I visited, for instance, he was always a welcoming host, making modest but tasty meals for us, having the towels set out, the guest bed made up. He stayed in touch with all of us, his children, by letters and phone calls. More important, he had made arrangements himself within a year of Mother's death to go to an ecclesiastical retirement community in California (a place he couldn't have considered before she died—the mention of it made her audibly, visibly, grit her teeth: she would *not* grow old and die among ministers and missionaries!).

Some of the reason he was going to Denver now was as a stopgap measure on the way to California: there was a wait list for Pilgrim Place that was two or three years long, and he had agreed with us that he needed sooner than that to be more with other people and to have more help in daily living. There was a new 'elderly complex' being developed near my sister, one she and her husband had hoped his parents might move to also. We had proposed it to Dad for the interim, and he agreed.

My sister and I were the ones in the family who had seen this as necessary; neither of my brothers felt there was a problem with Dad. And in general when I'd expressed my concern for him, she was the one of my siblings who responded. She and I had also been the ones who sorted through and distributed Mother's possessions after she died. She and I had divided up Dad's things this spring in anticipation of his move. She was expecting him out west in any case in the fall, after his summer in New Hampshire. It seemed natural to turn to her now, to ask her in effect to welcome him this much earlier than she'd planned, to watch out for him until he seemed all right again or until there was someone in New Hampshire—both my brothers were planning to visit him that summer—who could be, in some sense, responsible for him.

When I called her and proposed this, she agreed instantly. Quickly we worked out a division of labor. He would come to her, and she would either send him back later on his own or bring him back, depending on how he seemed, on how completely he recovered from this episode. Over the next few days I would get to New Jersey and take care of the last details in the house, figure out what to do with his car, still in his garage there, fetch the dog, and deal with the vanished van. Done.

26

The next day I presented the plan to him, mildly, casually. 'Tell you what, Dad: why don't I . . . ?'

Dad would have none of it. He was dismissive—politely dismissive, of course—but absolute: No. No. Of course I couldn't do all that. There was no need. He'd be on his way; the van would turn up; he'd take the bus home, or fly, and manage everything. No need to trouble myself.

I tried several more times, but I couldn't make a dent. At some point during the day I had my sister call him and invite him out to her house in Denver, just for a little rest after this exhausting spring. His responses to her as I heard them on my end were much the same as what he'd said to me. Oh, no, that was too much trouble. There was no need. He'd had a lovely rest at Sue's, wouldn't head home until he felt really restored. He couldn't, wouldn't, ask her to go to so much trouble.

I suppose what I hoped was that I could wear him down eventually. In any case, I kept at it on and off through the day. It would have been funny, I think, to anyone overhearing us—each of us being so scrupulously polite to the other, bowing and scraping verbally, but each stubbornly, absolutely persistent.

'Why don't you think about . . . ?'

'No, no, it's far too much . . .'

'Dad, I really think you should . . .'

'That's very kind, but I couldn't . . .'

And so on. We were too temperamentally alike in this regard to make any progress at all.

It became clear to me that I would need to be honest and forceful or he would never accede to me. That I would need to insist. I had never insisted on anything with my father. I don't know that anyone had.

The moment arrived later in the afternoon. My husband had wanted to be around for moral support when I made my move, and he was home. We were all in the kitchen, and Dad began again to say how kind we had been, how much trouble he'd caused, and how he thought certainly the next day he ought to get going.

I said I didn't think he ought to go to New Jersey alone. That I didn't want him to. I thought he should go to Denver.

My husband concurred.

Dad pointed out that there was an awful lot to do in New Jersey. He needed to be there. He wanted to get clear of it and get up to New Hampshire for the summer.

I told him I would handle the details in New Jersey.

He couldn't let me, he said.

The back door was open, and in the silences between us we could hear the music of someone in the apartment building behind us, the voices of people next door, the wind in the trees.

He brought up the dog again.

I said I would get the dog; I would find a

28

place for her until he came back east.

He certainly couldn't let me do that, he said. He'd been enough of a bother already. Though he was still characteristically polite, there was anger now—very contained, very submerged—in his voice.

I took a breath. 'Dad, I can't let you go,' I said. My heart was pounding in my ears.

'I'm afraid you have to.' He smiled a thin smile.

'No, Dad, I can't. You've been ill, really. You've had a kind of breakdown of some sort . . .'

There was a terrible silence. My husband ended it, offering his general support of me, making the argument again. Dad, as ever more willing to listen to men, nodded and seemed to consider what he was saying, but he still did not agree, did not say yes.

He and I were sitting opposite each other at the kitchen table. I had been looking sideways while my husband talked, out the window at the blur of leaves in the late-afternoon sun. Now I focused on Dad. I leaned forward toward him. 'Dad, listen. Imagine if the positions were reversed,' I said. 'If I had shown up at your house, and I was exhausted and seeing things that weren't there.' Now it was his turn to look away. 'You would feel it was your responsibility, your duty, to be sure I was all right, wouldn't you?' I waited a moment. 'You would never, never let me go off alone again right away. Would you?'

There was another long silence in which I think he saw his position clearly—and I saw it too, for the first time. He understood and we understood: we were taking the first step into his illness, whatever it was, together. We would be in charge of him now.

It was over in a few seconds. He looked back at me, then down. 'No,' he said quietly. 'No, you're right. I wouldn't let you go.'

\*　　　\*　　　\*

The next day, my husband bought him an overnight bag, loaned him a fresh shirt, and we drove him to the airport and sent him off to Denver, a small, thin, oddly dressed elderly man, still wearing his beloved horrible hat.

I flew to Newark airport, got a bus from there to Princeton, and then a cab from what is euphemistically called 'downtown' to Dad's house in the woods. I spent some hours there, bagging trash and odd possessions, packing up the last few things, vacuuming, cleaning the kitchen and bathrooms. It was awful to me, pathetic, to see the way he'd been living—no furniture, a mattress on the floor to sleep on, dog hairs everywhere.

By midafternoon I'd done what I could. I got in Dad's car and fetched his dog, Naomi, from the kennel. I drove to Connecticut and left the dog at Dad's sister's house there; she had offered to take her. I got home long after dark and parked the car in a willing neighbor's driveway until my sister and Dad could pick it up.

I spent much of the next day on the telephone. The van had turned up—at last!—and been towed to a nearby garage in western Massachusetts. I talked to the people in the rental office in New Jersey about their perhaps going up to get it for a surcharge. No deal. Finally I arranged to have it driven back down by a guy at the garage. He understood exactly how much at his mercy I was. He charged me a blackmail rate and kept me on the phone a long time. He said he loved my voice, he'd love to meet me, what did I look like, what was I wearing? I was very, very polite to him because I felt I had to be, but it seemed the final, almost laughably irrelevant unpleasantness to get through.

On schedule, though, we left for our stay in France; Dad came back east a few weeks later with my sister and had his summer in New Hampshire.

*     *     *

That fall I had a fellowship in writing at the MacDowell Colony in New Hampshire. We didn't have phones in our studios there, so I was sitting in the public phone closet under its single bright light, the voices and laughter of

31

the other fellows in the main room only slightly muffled by its closed door, when I learned from my sister what I already knew in my heart—that Dad had been diagnosed with what is called 'probable Alzheimer's disease.'

## CHAPTER THREE

In 1907, a German doctor in Frankfurt named Alois Alzheimer wrote an article on a mental patient of his, a woman who had died at fifty-six after a strange five-year illness.

Her first symptom had been paranoia, a suspiciousness of her own husband. Then, rapidly, that became entwined with profound memory impairment:

> She could no longer orient herself in her own dwelling, dragged objects here and there and hid them, and at times, believing that people were out to murder her, started to scream loudly.

She was institutionalized. It was difficult, Alzheimer said, to examine her, she was so confused, so frightened: 'She bursts into loud screams each time she is approached.' For a while she was still able to speak—at least to name objects, albeit with difficulty. Gradually, though, she declined: 'General imbecility keeps progressing.' By the time of her death, he described her as 'totally dulled, lying in bed with legs drawn up, incontinent.'

He performed an autopsy at the request of the director of the asylum, in part because no one could understand what had happened, what had gone wrong with this patient. What he discovered only increased the mystery. Her brain was riddled with neurofibrils, thickened and changed in a way that made them chemically unrecognizable. In places they were clustered together in what he called *thick bundles.* In addition, scattered over the entire cortex was a 'peculiar substance' that he was, again, unable to recognize chemically. He felt he was looking at a new disease, a mental illness with no name.

Now we call it by *his* name, Alzheimer's disease, and it is the dread disease of our time, particularly for those of us who are turning fifty, or sixty-five, or seventy and have escaped the *other* diseases one used to die of. It affects five million Americans and is the fourth leading cause of death among us. This is what was wrong with Dad, the answer I hadn't known to the questions the people who cared about him kept asking me.

It was called *probable* Alzheimer's disease in his case because at that time the only sure diagnosis was by autopsy, after death. Now we know of several genes that predispose to it, some with near certainty, so DNA testing would be a possible diagnostic tool. *Would be,* but isn't often—first because it's expensive; and second, because there's a sense in which for the patient, already afflicted, it's useless. Even now, fifteen years after Dad was diagnosed, there's nothing to offer someone with this disease except a few palliatives.

When I heard what was wrong with Dad, I experienced a strange rush of relief, a feeling that I think was related to the sense I'd had, for some years, of being responsible for him. I'd been single when my mother died, of all four siblings I lived nearest, and he and I had wound up spending a lot of time together over the six years between her death and his diagnosis. In the summers, I had gone up to see him in New Hampshire nearly every weekend, usually stretching my visits out to three or four days. I tried to have at least one extended summer stay of several weeks or even a month with him also. He came to our house in Cambridge for at least half his holidays, and I frequently drove to New Jersey just to visit. We spoke often on the phone and wrote more often—I still have many of his letters to me. I had noticed his failing early on, but no one else in the family shared my perception. 'He's fine with *me*,' my brother would say, and I would feel accused of imagining things or of responding to Dad in a way that was somehow *responsible* for making him seem vague.

Actually, what was unique in our relationship, Dad's and mine, was that when we were together we were usually *alone* together. Unlike my siblings, who all had spouses and multiple younger children, I had only one child, and at that stage Ben spent some of his free time with his own father and most of his summers at camp. When Dad and I saw each other, we were able to talk intimately, leisurely—about our lives, our family's story, our work. In the years after he retired, we labored together side by side for weeks and months, each summer and fall, redoing the ruin of a house he'd bought in New Hampshire. I honestly think I saw the workings of his mind more clearly than my siblings did at that stage. Certainly I saw his oddness, when he was odd, more sharply. But even I didn't really *want* to confront it. It came and went anyway, and so again and again I was able to argue myself out of acknowledging it.

But there came a point when I knew I had to try to do something about what I felt. I'd seen it once too often, too clearly. His friends, his last living sister, had begun to ask their questions. I felt the burden—as the one who thought something was wrong myself; as the one who seemed to be held responsible by others; and, after all, as the oldest daughter in the family, the one who saw him most—to do something.

I moved in slow motion, it must be said,

given who Dad was and, probably no less, who I was.

First I tried to talk to him about it—about depression, for instance, which seemed a possible explanation. About medication. He was characteristically vague in response (he could be more effectively nonresponsive than anyone I've ever known), and I felt he might be telling me, in essence, that it was none of my damned business.

Maybe that was true, I don't know. Certainly I was always able to shift quickly to thinking so, to feeling as guilty for trying to do something as for doing nothing—because while I didn't want to be irresponsible, I didn't want to be intrusive either. I remember writing once to his sister, my aunt Grace, that it seemed wrong to insist to Dad that he needed to have a particular *kind* of old age: as long as he was *all right*, why shouldn't he be sad sometimes, or scatty, or even not as tidy and fastidious as he once was? When I reported to my older brother that Dad wore the same clothes over and over in New Hampshire, Bob said, 'Hell, *I* wear the same clothes over and over in New Hampshire!' and I thought, Yes, yes, that was right; we're *all* slobs up there; I was being foolish again.

But the question now was, *was* he all right? When his friends asked me that, I felt a sense of guilt that I didn't know for certain one way or the other and that I wasn't being aggressive enough about finding out.

Okay: shamefacedly, then, I took the next step. I poked into his medicine chest when I was visiting and made a list of the contents so I could talk to my own doctor about what they might be, what they might mean. But there was mystification here too. For instance: Dad had a medicine my doctor told me was an antidepressant. That made me hopeful that he'd gone to his doctor himself, that he'd been diagnosed, that he was being treated. For a while—perhaps six months—I relaxed. But when I checked his medicine chest again, the bottle was still at the same level, nearly full. Now, what did *that* mean? Had he been taken off the medication? Did he have something else for depression that he kept elsewhere? Had he simply forgotten to take it or decided on his own he didn't want to, didn't need to? That would have been exactly like him. And once again, it was impossible to find out anyway, given the kind of nonresponse he made to my direct questions.

At a later point, feeling like a snoop, a spy— a criminal, really—I actually called his doctor without his knowledge to make a plea for information. His doctor: the name on the medicine bottles.

But no, he wasn't Dr. Nichols's doctor anymore; he hadn't seen him for several years. Though he had noticed some memory loss before then.

37

Did he know, then, who my father was seeing now?

No idea, he said.

I went back to Dad again and tried to pierce the thicket of proud (or was it only confused?) obfuscation. Finally I got another name. I called him. This man *had* seen Dad, within the year. He had prescribed some medications, yes, but he thought Dad was in good shape. He didn't know him well enough to comment on memory loss.

I felt utterly stymied at this point. It seemed, in the end, that unless Dad was willing—or able—to talk to me honestly and openly about his health, there was almost nothing I could do.

What I *did* do, finally, was to pressure him to change his circumstances. To urge him, with my sister's support—she was, as I've said, the one who listened to me, who seemed to be willing to believe there was something wrong—to move.

And now he had moved, and my sister, living ten minutes away from him, guiding him into his new life, had found him a new doctor, had insisted on starting out with thorough exams, and had given us all a diagnosis. It was real. It could be named. It was Alzheimer's disease. And I felt my guilty relief to know it.

In my own defense, I'll say that this was born in part of ignorance: I didn't really know much about the disease and the details of its terrible course. And in any case, the relief was mixed, of course, with real sorrow for Dad. But the diagnosis signaled the end to the nameless anxiety that I'd felt had been mine alone for years, and for that, no matter what, I was grateful.

*     *     *

My father's obituary in 1991 said that he died of Alzheimer's disease. Of course, no one, strictly speaking, dies of Alzheimer's disease. They die of other things, horrible things that happen to them because they *have* Alzheimer's disease. Sherwin B. Nuland in *How We Die* lists some of the possibilities and details their agonies: starvation, because you've forgotten how to eat; pneumonia, because you've forgotten how to walk, how to sit, and your lungs suffer for that; also urinary-tract infections and septic decubitus ulcers. This last is what Dr. Alzheimer's original patient died of, eventually—bedsores: 'lying in bed with legs drawn up, incontinent . . . despite all care, [she] developed decubiti.'

My father had his own version of death-by-Alzheimer's, and I watched it slowly overtake him without realizing what was happening, without knowing I was witnessing the approach of the end—something else to feel guilty about, since he was in my care again when he died, living forty minutes from Boston

39

in what is called a 'continuing care facility' named Sutton Hill Village. It had turned out, once he was diagnosed, that he could not go on from Denver to the ecclesiastical community he'd chosen in California; they had no arrangements for dealing with Alzheimer's disease there. He decided that when he got to the stage in which he couldn't live alone anymore, even with the very elaborate support systems my sister had set in place, he would come back east to live near me. I'd found Sutton Hill and we'd gone to look at it together on one of his visits to me when he was still fairly intact. And when a space opened for him in the fall of 1988, it was my sister's turn to feel relief; to send him back to me.

I watched him, then, and tried to help him, as he moved from being a fairly functional person to a completely incompetent one. I was, as they say, 'in charge' of him as he moved through some of the more humiliating and degrading stages of the disease. Part of what I want to record here is how that felt, how I reacted, certainly not using myself as a model of any sort but simply as an example.

Throughout my father's disease, I struggled with myself to come up with the helpful response, the loving response, the ethical response. I wanted to give him as much of myself as I could. But I also wanted, of course, to have my own life. I wanted, for instance, to be able to work productively. I wanted not to let my sorrow and despair over Dad color my daily relations with my husband or my contact with my son, who was by then in college. There were many books, and I read a few, to tell me how to approach all this, and I had joined a support group of caregivers well before Dad arrived to be near me. There I heard many of the same things I'd also read: that I shouldn't feel guilty about sometimes not liking Dad, that I should make a special effort to get out often and see friends, that I should take care of my personal needs, that I should turn to others for help, that I should revisit old hobbies and pastimes to give me a lift.

None of this seemed to connect with the feelings I had. I thought of most of it, honestly, as irrelevant at best, condescending at worst. The truth was that not even directly as advice was it apt for me. I was, in almost every sense, *lucky* as a caregiver. The strains I felt were not that Dad required too much of my time, or even—as was the case for some people in my caregivers group—that he might drain my financial resources. Dad had good care at Sutton Hill. He really *needed* very little of my time, in that sense. And he had enough money of his own to get through a very long haul with the illness—a combination of Social Security, retirement benefits from decades at two large universities, a ministerial pension, and the invested proceeds from the sale of his house.

What's more, he wasn't 'difficult.' In

41

everything, he wished to be as little trouble as possible. For as long as he could, he acceded to every rule made for him, complied with every restriction—and never complained.

Still, it was hard. Not just hard, it was awful. Yet my first task as I understood it was not to let Dad see I felt this way. I wanted, while I could, to make our time together lighthearted, fun, interesting, as he had always sought to make our times together when he was in charge of me. I wanted to give him respite from his awareness—diminishing awareness, to be sure—that he was ill and would only get worse. That he was, in effect, incarcerated and would never get out. That he was dying, and dying in what was to me—and to him too, I imagine—the worst way possible.

I struggled with myself nearly every time I visited him over how to respond, what to say, what to do. It was all the small decisions, and nearly none of the big ones, that confounded and occasionally dumbfounded me. Even now I don't know what things I would have done differently—or *how* I'd do them differently if I did. My particular version of the caregiver's dilemma, then, was one of confusion: moral confusion, emotional confusion, ethical confusion, practical confusion.

Example: a walk in the woods with Dad. I called him ahead of time at Sutton Hill early one morning, approaching this with a frisson of anxiety: I knew he often thought the phone was some sort of fire alarm or doorbell and got agitated trying to respond. Those times when he did remember how to pick up the receiver, it wasn't unusual for him simply to hold it, having forgotten what came next; and if he successfully got to the next stage and actually lifted it to his ear, he often had it reversed, the earpiece at his mouth. So if I heard a silence on the line now after the pickup, my strategy was to *bellow. Dad? Dad, hello, I'm on the phone! Hello, it's me, Sue! Don't hang up! Turn the phone around, Dad. Hello, Dad? hello, hello!*

Sometimes it worked. This morning I had finally gotten through and told him I was coming out to visit him. He was pleased. He sounded eager.

By the time I arrived, though, about an hour later, he'd already forgotten all that and was clearly completely surprised to see me. Delighted—'Why, Sue!'—but surprised.

I suggested we go to Great Meadows, an Audubon sanctuary on the Concord River twenty minutes or so away—we'd taken walks there often—and he was enthusiastic. I helped him to change into hiking boots and we signed out and left.

We were well past the cluster of commercial civilization near Sutton Hill—the shops, the gas station, the motel—when I realized that I was going to need to pee at some point fairly soon. Stupid not to have used Dad's lavatory, I thought. But in the past I'd noticed rustic rest rooms off the parking lot at Great Meadows. That would do, I told myself now, and we drove on, talking desultorily, catching each other upon our 'news.' Mine was the same news I always delivered: how my book was coming, how my husband's book was coming, how Ben was, *where* Ben was—which was, variably during these years, South America, Africa, France, or Harvard. Dad's news was always fresh and astonishing, straight from his disordered brain. Hallucinatory visits from my long-dead mother or his parents or friends. Odd dreamlike parties or events he *claimed* he'd attended. I'll hit the rest rooms as soon as we get there, I was thinking, as I took in the latest installment of his biochemical adventures.

We turned into the long wooded driveway. Through the trees, the river glittered in the sun. It was cool out, breezy: a beautiful day for a walk. We wove our way down to the gravel lot, where only one other car was parked. No one was around. The shed with the rest rooms in it stood in a clearing up a short trail from the parking area.

I pulled into a space and cut the engine. I looked over at Dad, waiting patiently, sweetly, passively as ever in the passenger seat for the next move to be indicated.

I suddenly realized that I had no idea how to handle this. If we got out of the car now and

44

I told him to stay there while I went to the rest room, he might well forget why he was waiting in the two or three minutes it would take me to go. The reasonless impulse to wander—which I thought of roughly as a voice saying to him, 'It's time for you to get going'—might come over him, and those few minutes could be just long enough for him to get so lost in these woods that I wouldn't be able to find him; he was still a good walker, a brisk walker.

I couldn't risk it. I couldn't do it. We sat there.

For a moment I considered taking him to the rest room with me. I could station him outside the stall, assuming there was a stall; or outside the door, which I could leave ajar. *Stay right there*, I could say, as you would say to a child. I could keep up a running conversation, calling for a steady series of responses, so I'd be warned if he took even a few steps away. But this was too crudely intimate, too undignified. Perhaps not for me, but for him.

No, here's what it was: for my *idea* of him. In any case, I didn't feel I could do it.

Then it occurred to me: I could lock him in the car!

He had enormous trouble with mechanical devices: on-off knobs, electrical outlets, handles, the telephone or radio. He was sitting there now because he hadn't ever mastered opening the door to my Saab—the handle was in a different place and worked differently

45

from the handle in his old Volvo. Occasionally he'd start to fumble uselessly around, and then I would reach across and open the door for him. Or sometimes I came around and opened it for him from the outside. Most of the time he just sat there waiting for one or the other, as he was doing now.

What I was thinking was that I could say, 'I'll be back in a minute, Dad,' lock my door as I left, and come up quietly on his side and lock his too. Even if he forgot he was waiting for me, even if he heard the siren call to walk, to walk anywhere, he'd never figure out the combined problem of the handle and the door's lock in time. And it would be for the sake of our walk, our promised morning out, that I would be doing this. For his sake too, for his safety.

But almost as soon as I had it, I dismissed this idea. I couldn't, I just *couldn't*, lock my father in. There was no activity, no pleasure I could offer him, that was worth my calculatedly relying on his incapacity.

I was furious with myself now for my stupidity. For having put us in a situation where I had to make this decision. I felt a sense of shame for even having thought of this solution, for being the kind of person who could have stopped to figure out that it would work. I felt like kicking something.

I got out. I let Dad out. We took a short hurried walk, one tenth the time we usually spent here.

Maybe he didn't notice. Certainly he didn't complain when I led him back to the car, when we drove away. And I don't think he saw the roadside stand where we usually stopped and loaded up on treats for him to take back— fresh fruit, a bag of peanuts, a small square or two of homemade fudge. I hope not. Back at Sutton Hill, I used the ladies' room, and before I said goodbye we took another walk, longer and slower, around the too-civilized, too-familiar grounds.

I still don't know what would have been right. If I'd been a different kind of person, more straightforward, more blunt perhaps, I might have said, 'I'm going to the bathroom, Dad, and I'm going to lock the car in case you forget for a minute what you're doing here.' Sometimes, when I had to, I managed such honesty about his failings. ('Uh-oh, Dad, you forgot to zip your fly.') More often, though, I didn't. More often I tried to hold on to my sense of who he had been, to keep connecting to *that* version of Dad, even as it slowly changed and disappeared.

Why?

I suppose partly so he could hold on to it as long as possible too. Maybe just to make our time together easier, more pleasurable. But part of it may have been denial also, a kind of selfish and uncourageous wish not to have to acknowledge everything that was happening to

47

him: *Don't make me see that, Dad. Don't make me have to know.*

In any case, today my fastidiousness for some or all of these reasons had made impossible what might have been a pleasure for him. And I couldn't understand, I still can't, all the elements that lay in the balance. Whether I was serving the dignity I wanted to hold on to in him—that I wanted *him* to hold on to—or just some misguided notion of myself, the notion that I was the sort of person who wouldn't *think* of doing the very thing I'd just thought of doing.

I don't know. But I remember feeling in the car on the way home, and telling my husband later on, that I was perhaps the worst prepared temperamentally of any of my siblings to be caring for my father as he sank into this terrible illness.

\*     \*     \*

Even as my father had his own version of the Alzheimer's death, he had his own version of the disease itself, very different from many of the ones I'd read about. He was able until very late in the course of things to present a relatively intact surface to those he was comfortable with and whose references he could follow. He held on to much of his vocabulary, though structuring it was sometimes hard. He retained his long-term memory longer than most sufferers do, so that he could connect with people from his past—and with me and my brothers and sister—until the end of his life. He retained, too, the graciousness that had always marked him. Sometimes, in fact, this became an impediment to understanding him, as he circumnavigated with great effort and invention some routine polite exchange, just because he couldn't quite remember the normal short form for it. On a bad day, 'You're welcome,' could take several incoherent minutes.

Of course, the basic trajectory of the disease was always there, underlying all this and having its way with Dad's brain. I could watch him from week to week and month to month take the next step, and then another, along its inevitable downward curve.

But the point is, it left some recognizable things behind, as it does with most sufferers. Things that mark one victim from the next, though it still may take someone who knew him *before* to recognize him. The mother of a man in my support group, for instance, held on to her characteristic stubbornness as she grew more and more ill. His exchanges with her came to consist mostly of her telling him what she would not ever *ever* do as he was trying to persuade her she had to do it. The group would make one suggestion or another about how to manage her, and he'd shake his head

49

almost proudly and say, 'She'll never go for it.'

The mother of a friend of mine, always a little spacey and whimsical, grew more and more otherworldly as she descended into the disease, becoming, in effect, a gracious but slightly demented angel.

So too with my father, the disease oddly intensified—or maybe just laid bare—who he really was. Even when he was deeply gone into it, the phrases of self-effacement rose easily to his lips. 'Oh, don't bother.' 'That's too much trouble.' 'You shouldn't have to do that.' His dying itself was quiet and undemanding—no great drama, not much suffering, I believe. A kind of final self-effacement.

Still, by the time he died, he was nearly destroyed. To those around him at Sutton Hill, those who hadn't known him before, he must have seemed sometimes a horror, sometimes a bad joke. There were times when he seemed like one or the other of these things even to me, who *had* known him, who loved him.

I think that for others in my family, who didn't see him at the end, who didn't witness his slow decline, he may live intact in memory, much as he was before his illness. I hope so. But that isn't true for me. It was in part to exorcise my final haunting images of my father that I wanted to look at, to explain, the way he fragmented and lost himself in his illness; and who he was before it. And, as I've said, to talk about the way I dealt with what had happened and how it felt. But along the way, while I was working on what I hoped would be my *useful* memoir—reconstructing my father again for myself, imagining him whole, putting together the pieces that slowly disintegrated and broke off—I found there were still things I could learn from him, still things he could teach me, things that helped bring him home in my own memory from the faraway land of his disease.

This book is in some ways, of course, a test of *my* memory, of my ability to construct and reconstruct events and lives and histories. There's an element of discomfort here for me. It isn't just my awareness that the way I see my father may not be the way others see him; that's inevitable. Neither is it the fear that I may get some things *wrong*, though I have that fear, and of course, I surely will. Rather it has to do, I think, with the variable nature of memory itself and with its role in my family, for my parents—my father *and* my mother— and for me.

My father was a historian, a church historian. It makes his illness a bitter irony. But the irony was there in another form even before he became ill, for he was someone who seemed to have almost no interest in his own history, his personal history. He spoke only rarely of his own memories of childhood or youth, and then never at length. And I don't think he *used* his personal memories in coming to understand himself. In that sense, in the sense that we mean it in contemporary post-Freudian America, I don't think he *did* understand himself. (He knew his Freud, of course. He jokingly said to me once that he was a prime example of what repression could accomplish. He was speaking, I think, both of his inability to recollect much from his early life—even, really, to think about it—and of his energetic, virtually nonstop professional output.)

What we knew of his history we knew mostly from his sisters and his stepmother. He seemed disconnected from it. He had no recollection, for example, of his own mother, though he was eight when she died. None. This seems extraordinary to me. Repression indeed. And he couldn't call up any of those little incidents from childhood that my mother specialized in. I can remember once repeating a story to him that my grandmother—his stepmother—had told me: that two or three years after she'd married his widowed father, my father, a boy of thirteen or fourteen then, idly asked her one day whether she had any insanity in her family. She was startled. She said no, no, she didn't, and asked him why he'd wanted to know. 'Just wondering,' he said casually, and walked away. When I repeated this to him, he laughed in delight—as though it were utterly fresh to him; as though it were about someone else, some other wiseass early adolescent.

'But did you ask that?' I said.

And his answer was something like, Well, I suppose I must have.

'*Dad!*' I protested. 'Did you or didn't you?' What I wanted to know, I suppose, was whether he remembered the impulse to be that nasty, that snide.

But I never found out. Either he knew and wasn't saying or he simply didn't remember. I'd bet money on the second.

My mother was utterly different. She remembered everything about her past. She loved her own history, every detail of it. She suffered from it and reveled in it until the day she died. She could weep at sixty for a slight she suffered at six or sixteen. She could recollect forever the fabric and cut of a dress she wore on a triumphal evening in high school, or the compliment someone paid her in college. Or the insult.

She used her memory to define herself. It was her life and it was her weapon, sometimes her bludgeon. I remember one summer afternoon the year before she died, her haranguing my visiting grandparents, then in their eighties, poor things, about a decision they made to send her away to camp when she was twelve. She spoke of it as if it had happened the day before, as if it were an expulsion from a kind of Eden. She got teary. 'It was *hell*!' she cried out. And I remember that in the midst of all this, as my grandfather

53

tried to slow her down—'No doubt we made mistakes'—my grandmother, a vague smile on her lips, discreetly but deliberately reached up and turned off her hearing aid.

My mother wrote poetry—lyric poetry, of course. And that concentrated focus on one's own feelings, one's own remembered agony and despair and joy, marked her personality as it marked her work. It was terrifying to me as a child—and something I resist in myself and others as an adult—that insistence on high drama, that inability to let go of or to integrate painful memory. It was why I sought refuge then in my father's calm, his forgetfulness of self, if that's what it was. It may be part of why I now write fiction, why I choose to move around imaginatively in other, invented people's joys and agonies. And it may also be why my own memory is so spotty. Why it so often comes at things from an angle.

My first memory of my father, for instance, is not truly of him but of his absence. Actually, it's one of my first clear memories of any kind. My earlier recollections are fragmentary, odd home movies that show only an out-of-context scene or two before breaking off and flickering dark. This memory, though, is sharp and clear—it has meaning for me as well as detail. And the meaning is that my father has left us; he's gone away.

This was the scene: I was five. My father was in Germany for a long stay, a half-year stay. On a warm early summer's day, a friend of my parents came to take pictures of us—of my mother and my younger sister and baby brother and me—to send to him. Peculiarly, I can remember clearly the chair we sat in to be photographed. It was painted a bright blue. It had been set out in the backyard for this session. The backyard was a communal one, behind several apartment buildings on the south side of Chicago in the university neighborhood—Hyde Park. The yard was hard-packed dirt for the most part, worn barren by the play of all the children who used it daily. The chair looked strange to me, out of place and *wrong*, plopped down out there.

What I remember most of the picture taking was the sense of yearning connection I felt, thinking of my father as I looked straight into the camera. Thinking of my picture, but not me, going to him, far across the ocean. He had been away at that point for three or four months—he'd left soon after my baby brother was born—and would be gone about three months more.

My memory, then, is not really of him but of the effort of trying to construct him in my mind, of struggling to imagine him, of missing him. My memory is of memory, working to find its object.

There were perhaps a dozen or so photographs from that day in one of our family albums. I still have two or three—the pictures were divided up after my mother's death and distributed evenly among us. In them my sister and I look strained, solemn and tired. We'd recovered only a month or so earlier from chicken pox. In one of the pictures of me holding David—he seems almost too big for me to be holding safely, but I am—you can still see the shadow of several pockmarks sprinkled on my face. The photographer was someone we children didn't know well, and that's on my face too: a shyness, a reserve. I'm not smiling.

It's easy, of course, to read too much into the accidents that are family snapshots. We were, after all, normal, bright children, well cared for, every nuance of our development noted and described in the long letters my mother wrote to her mother—which were then circulated through my mother's large family and have come back, after all these years, to me. But I think these pictures of us as grave, cautious children reveal something. I think they speak of a certain aspect, anyway, of my family's life. Because my mother—who was alone with us that summer—didn't take much joy in us as children. We were too much her life's work, her project. She reserved her vivacity, her charm, which could he enormous, for other adults. Those same long letters that chronicled our growth described all her labors on our behalf. These labors were ceaseless, and although in the letters they were described cavalierly, as though she undertook them gracefully and lightly, there was another note struck in her later written recollections and in her poetry—the grim note of enduring her fate, bitterly enduring it. Blaming my father, blaming us, for our existence, for the *work* we made for her. And this is more the note we were aware of at the time, the note that made me, as a child, cautious, careful not to anger her, not to ask for too much. Never to be a *bother*.

It was my father who brought gaiety and fun to our lives. This isn't fair to my mother, of course. He didn't have that endless round of chores connected to us to wear him down. He wasn't responsible in the world's view, or in his own, for how we looked, how we behaved, how we did in school. But it wasn't simply a matter of the division of labor. It was temperament too. He was by nature patient and attentive. He saw the humor in small things. He was charmed and amused by his children—by most children, in fact. He was steady; he was emotionally reliable.

My mother wasn't, then or ever. Speaking her name—'Mama . . .'—could bring, unpredictably, any one of a variety of responses. Loving: 'Yes, Susie?' Or frantic: 'What! What *is* it? What do you want?' Or just: '*Will* you children leave me alone for one minute?' and then tears, tears. Her pleasures were all in turning away from us, in privacy. The cigarettes and coffee lingered over when

57

we'd dispersed after breakfast, the crossword puzzles, the endless games of solitaire, the mystery novels, with their lurid and—to me—compelling covers. Illness was something she particularly cherished. She could shut her door. She could rest. She could ask my father for help. Her letters are full of it, the lavish, loving descriptions of the latest thing that's gone wrong with her body.

My father was the one who played with us. Who wrestled, who sang goofy songs. Who read to us as we all jammed together on the couch in his study. Who took us to special events. But most of all it was he who was attentively, evenly, perhaps a little abstractedly too, *always the same.* He was safety.

It was my father who was gone when these pictures were taken. And I think that is the source of the tension I see in my sister's face and mine, of the caution and reserve we project while we freeze ourselves, while we sit still—so still now!—for the strange kind man taking the pictures, whoever he was; and for our father, waiting to see us in a distant country.

\*       \*       \*

I would guess, actually, that my mother was relatively happy during this period. There was no baby who pleased her more than my gentle-tempered, easy, fat little brother. During my

58

father's absence, she had found a house for sale in the neighborhood and it seemed we could afford it. Perhaps soon we could move out of the apartment where four children and two adults lived in five rooms. The letters written by her in this period are full of that: color schemes, curtains, who would be put where. And of course there was the pulling together of finances to make it happen: loans, mortgages, income from possible boarders. These were things that made her feel competent, things she enjoyed.

But she had emerged from a deep depression only the year before, and though none of her children remembers that episode specifically, I think that for all of us its symptoms—the profound retreat from us into sorrow, the sound of weeping behind a closed door, the sudden tearful recoil from what seemed a harmless remark—these were already part of who she was for us, happy for the moment or no.

The child I was then questioned none of this. My mother was who she was; my father was gone. But it seems strange to me now, almost unimaginable: my father left my mother for six months. He left a depressive woman of twenty-nine with four children under seven to take care of, one of them only a few weeks old. Left her to go with a group of professors to Germany on a mission to help help the postwar university system there, decimated by the flight and murder of Jews and resisters. Left her to travel after the academic year was done through Italy, Switzerland, and France, meeting with colleagues, looking at art and documents of interest to him in his work. And left us waiting for his safe return to our lives. I didn't think of it, of course, until years later, how much he must have *wanted* to go.

This is my memory then: the blue chair, the hot day, the big happy baby balanced on my lap, the stranger with the camera. This is the way I have to tell this story, moving from these details into my parents' lives, my father's history. Into *how it was* for us. And all the while I feel behind me, over my right shoulder and my left, the sense of both of my parents, of how differently they would tell it, of how different the terms are in which they understood it and felt it. Of how my representation itself makes the story mine, not hers or his. But uneasy and unsure as I sometimes feel as I call up the memories and the words to cast them in, I am the one who has the need to do it.


## CHAPTER FOUR

Was the chair blue? As I look at it in the black-and-white photos I still have, I think not,

60

actually. I think it was a desk chair of my father's, the wood stained dark. I think the blue chair must have been another, later, chair, and I'm confusing the two. But I wonder why. Is it my unconscious impulse as a writer to get at the *blueness* of the two little girls who miss their father? Could I be that corny? It's possible, I suppose, though it's not fun to think so.

Was the ceiling in my father's study in our Chicago house really papered with silver stars in a night sky when we moved in? And if it was, when did they disappear? Some things I'm just plain not sure of. Some I am. Could you not ride one stop past our house on the commuter train from downtown if you wanted to, and see it as you passed? See the windows at its back—my bedroom, my brothers'—the kitchen door, the sagging porch, the grapevine, the mulberry tree arched over the garage and the scraggly yard; see it all laid out as it must have appeared to those thousands and thousands of travelers who flashed by over the years we lived there, who never gave any of it a second thought? Yes. Yes, indeed you could.

This is the way those years come back to me. These images. And then sometimes a detail from them triggers a set of associations that calls up scene and dialogue and also, nearly simultaneously, a larger sense, an emotive sense. What we might call the sense of *how it was.* And if one or two small things are wrong, I let this go. It's the Proustian triggering action I'm grateful for. It's the *feeling* I want to get at.

When I write fiction I rearrange memory, I invent memory in order to make narrative sense of it for a reader and for myself, to explain why it's important—exactly *how it was.* If I have a call, I suppose it is that: to try to make meaning, to embody meaning, in the narrative arrangement of altered and invented bits of memory. To be compelled to do this, actually.

But in this case, in this book, I have to work differently. I have to rely purely on what happened as I remember it, and somehow to make narrative sense of that. This is harder. And it begs the question, Does life *make* narrative sense? Certainly we would like it to. Maybe the recent fin-de-siècle success of the memoir was an expression of that desire and a kind of resulting conviction: yes, it can. It can make sense. If I phrase it just right, look at it just right, it can.

But it's possible too, I think, that this wish to give life *narrative* coherence may he a substitute for all kinds of other more-or-less vanished beliefs about other kinds of coherence, beliefs about what life *means.* We're stuck now insisting that, at the very least, it ought to make a story; it ought to have a shape.

In any case, here is my father, in memory. Here, look at him, sitting in his study, almost in silhouette in front of the one window. He's a small handsome man, Semitic looking, which runs on the male side of his family—a strong down-curving nose, skin that shadows to olive. He has dark hair, hair he will keep until he dies, hair that will remain untouched by gray until much later in his life. He wears glasses when he works, and often a jacket and tie.

This was his room, the only room in the house that revealed much of anything about him. Three of the walls were nearly covered with bookshelves, the books in them an odd mixture of his professional library—these often in German or French and in any case of no interest at that time to me—and the books he and my mother read or had read for pleasure. His big desk, and even sometimes the floor around it, was always stacked with papers; one of the books he was writing while we lived on Harper Avenue, or student essays or bluebooks, or an article for the journal he edited, *Church History.* Framed pictures of figures he was interested in hung on the wall. I remember a sepia-toned photograph of the Swiss historian Jacob Burkhardt staring down from *his* desk, in *his* study. The door onto the hall was always open.

I think that open door drove my mother a

bit mad. She saw her role as protecting my father's privacy. If we came into the house with a bunch of friends, she was on guard: 'Don't you take all those children up there. Your father's working.' If we made it past her, she'd holler, 'Are you up there bothering your father?'

The study was physically at the heart of the house; the door faced the top of the only flight of stairs to the second floor. Whenever you came up—whoever came up—if you stepped just slightly forward out of your path to your own room, you could see him there at his desk. And he could see you.

As he watched the parade in the hallway, he always seemed mildly amused, tolerant of us all. You could actually hide in his study from others, and he would just raise his eyebrows for a moment and then go on with what he was doing. I think in fact he *chose* the open door. He seemed to enjoy the racket. Maybe this was because his protection against it was, in a sense, built in: he simply absented himself from whatever might interfere with his thoughts. It just didn't register.

My aunt Ellen, my father's oldest sister, once counted eighteen children in the house when she was visiting and noted that my father was undisturbed by it. In fact, he worked through it. Clearly the contrast with her own father was an important part of the delight she took in this—she, unlike my father, remembered my grandfather's intolerance of noise, of children, of any interruption in his sanctified routines.

For a while a little girl from down the street—Judith Kaplan, my younger brother's age—became infatuated with my father. Whenever she was over, she'd find her way eventually to his study. She'd stand by his desk—her head barely level with its surface—and watch him writing. Her question became famous in my family, the pesterer's question: 'Whatcha doin', Mister Nichols?'

And he *answered* her—that seemed even funnier to me. Politely, graciously, he told her, every time. 'Well, Judith,' he'd say, 'I'm trying to work.'

'Whatcha working on, Mister Nichols?'

Look at him again. This time I'm standing in Judith's place, a tall ungainly girl of twelve or thirteen, come to my father's study to complain to him of the biblical passage that says, 'For my yoke is easy, and my burden is light.'

I'm outraged by this and I want my father's confirmation of that outrage. I'm thinking of all that's required in Christian life, all that's insisted on—all the kinds of goodness, both of intention and behavior. The passage simply isn't true, is it, Pop? Hah! His yoke, *easy*? His burden *light*?

And my father says, well, it is and it isn't true. He knows what I mean; he knows a lot is

65

demanded, that there is a lot you must demand of yourself, if you are to be truly Christian. But with grace this may sometimes *feel* easy. Like a lifting up, he says. But of course it isn't easy in reality. No. He agrees. It isn't. I have a point.

And then he says maybe I should be thinking more about the words *yoke* and *burden*—they're there too, aren't they?—and less about the adjectives. Maybe then the passage won't bother me so much.

Another time: I arrive—at the age of fourteen—to tell my father that I won't be taking communion anymore. I've listened to the invitation to my first communion, calling on me to give my whole heart to the service of Christ and His kingdom, to serve the Lord and keep His commandments all the days of my life, and it has set me to wondering: *Do* I regret my sins?

Not enough of them, I know that. I'm aware, actually, that some of them even please me.

Do I love Jesus Christ? I don't know. I just don't know.

Am I in perfect charity with all men? I am not. And I'm not sorry about it, either. I have been a very *good* littler girl, shy and anxious to please, trapped between two more willful and attractively dynamic siblings. But being good has got me exactly nowhere. Now I've set about enjoying my resentments, my hatreds. I

66

cherish them, in fact. I think of myself as a hard case. It is, as I see it, what I have. All I have. To pretend I'm someone I'm not puts that at risk and takes something precious away from me, something even more precious than the comfort I've drawn from the sacrament. I tell my father I can't, in conscience, any longer participate.

My father has turned from whatever he was doing to listen to me in all my conscientious self-importance. This is his gift, this full, generous, disinterested attention. It is how he approaches everyone. After his death I will read a testimonial from a student of his describing his quiet, careful *listening* in his office hours, and I will recognize this extraordinary generosity. You never knew—never even had a sense of—what he put aside to give himself to your pressing concerns. But he was *there*. When you asked him to be, he was absolutely there.

Now my father says he's sorry I feel this way but he honors my decision. He says it's all right. I don't need to take communion right now. I should do what I think is right.

Instantly I feel a kind of retroactive rage. *It's all right?* 'But why did you make us go to Sunday school and confirmation classes and stuff if it doesn't matter?' So much of my precious little life, wasted.

He says it's not at all that it doesn't matter, just that I should make up my own mind. He

67

says that what he and my mother have wanted for all of us by giving us religious training is for the path to faith to be familiar to us. Later, he says, if my thinking changes—as he hopes it will—I'll know how to find my way back to believing, and to the church too.

*I won't,* I want to say. But then I'm aware again of that part of me that yearns for faith—and for my family, which seems so embedded in it. I stand there silent for a while—he waits—and then I ask my father whether he had a 'call.' I've read about calls; I certainly know the story of Paul. I have very much wanted a call myself, a sign from God that this is His world, that He wishes to claim me. It is in some measure feeling that no such thing is possible that has turned me away from whatever *believing* might otherwise have been for me now.

No, my father says, there was not a moment as such for him. It was far more gradual, far more the result of following steadily where his beliefs and feeling led him. And then he makes an analogy I have never forgotten. He compares faith to falling in love; and, more, he says that for him the experience of both was as though he'd entered a room backwards—backed into it—so that by the time he was able to look around and understand where he was, he was already encircled by it, *held* in it.

And I feel a doubled yawning sorrow enter my life. I'm so sure I'll never feel this way—

*encircled*, either by love or faith.

* * *

The study was also the room where my father read to us. He was a wonderful reader, taking all the parts in whatever the story was. He loved doing a falsetto for women and girls, *being* them and mocking them at the same time, something I would remember later when he was so easily contemptuous of the chirping cheerfulness of the mostly female residents of Sutton Hill. He read whatever we picked, without judgment or censure. He read *Winnie the Pooh* and *Treasure Island* and *Swiss Family Robinson*. He read the Laura Ingalls Wilder books, which I hated and my sister loved. He read *Stuart Little* and *Charlotte's Web*. All the classics, the approved texts. But he also read *Archie* comics and *Katie Keene* and *Little Lulu*. We all loved Lulu, and we especially loved the voice my father gave her: high-pitched and ridiculous, yes, but also somehow sturdily competent.

When my little brother was old enough for read-aloud books, he got to pick them, and we older children drifted away. We'd heard most of them several times by then anyway. But every once in a while, I'd go and sit on the daybed too, just for a few minutes, drawn by my father's voice. And often I'd listen to the story from my bedroom with my door open while I did my homework, not quite able to hear the words, but noting the changing inflections, Pooh to Piglet, Tubby to Lulu. He once did such a convincing and self-pitying Eeyore that it brought sudden tears to my eyes.

*     *     *

Where else do I see my father? Where else do I remember him clearly?

In Maine, of course, at my grandparents' camp—a group of small cabins scattered in a clearing in the woods by a pristine lake. We went there every long academic summer from the time I was three until I was in my teens (except for that summer my father was in Europe), and there was no part of that experience that wasn't stamped indelibly on my mind, my heart.

Even the long trips getting there. We would be packed in, three in the front seat, three in back, the luggage area and the top of the car overloaded with duffel bags of clothing for the whole summer, with diapers, with my father's papers and books, with food for the trip. There was always a dog too, standing across several laps or sitting on someone, hot and sticky, perspiration spooling down lavishly from his dangling tongue. The interstate highway system was only beginning to be developed, so it usually took us four or five days of slow meandering loops on two-lane roads, through small towns across the Midwest and then in Pennsylvania and across upper New York State, to get there. Someone was always carsick; someone else had to pee— *Now!* Someone had pinched someone, encroached on someone else's sacred sense of space, taken all the crayons, read over someone else's shoulder, *breathed* on someone too hard. As an adolescent I once asked to change seats because the wind was blowing my hair against my carefully arranged *do*. My mother grew frantic with all of us. She reached around, slapping people randomly; it didn't matter who, the person probably deserved it or would shortly. She smoked, she yelled, she wept.

In my recollection, my father never lost his temper. He kept us playing games. We sang along with him the hymns we all loved, several verses through. He sang to us his repertoire of nutty, naughty songs: 'Cocaine Bill and Morphine Sue,' 'There Were Three Jolly Fishermen,' and 'The Bulldog on the Bank'— whose lyrics were:

Oh, the bulldog on the bank
(BASSO)
And the bullfrog in the pool.
Oh, the bulldog on the bank
(BASSO PROFONDO)
And the bullfrog in the pool.

71

Oh, the bulldog on the bank
And the bullfrog in the pool . . .
The bulldog called the bullfrog
A *green old water fool!*

That was it. We loved it. Do it again, Pop.

There was 'Thirty Dirty Purple Birds,' spoken thus: Toity doity poiple boids, sittin' on a coibstone munchin' woims an choipin' an' boipin'. Along comes Goity, the goil with the coils and the poils, and her boyfriend Hoibie, what woiks in a shoit factory in Joizey. An' *they* saw the toity doity poiple boids sittin' on a coibstone munchin' woims an' choipin' and boipin', an' they was p'toibed.

Where did this come from, some old vaudeville routine? His days in Boy Scouts? Undergraduate nonsense at Yale? His resources for the ridiculous seemed endless.

One summer we borrowed two cars for the trip—a favor, actually, to friends who'd moved to Massachusetts and needed someone to drive the cars east for them. One was a medium-sized sedan. My mother drove this one, with the bags and three of us children and her high-pitched temper. The other an MG. We took turns riding in it one at a time with my father.

The MG was dark green. Its turn indicators were fingerlength arrows that dropped from either side of the car and pointed left or right. It had bucket seats upholstered in leather

72

whose smell somehow hinted at a kind of life completely unfamiliar to me. I have never been in a more satisfactory car. And my father seemed as at home in it as Stuart Little—or even Toad of Toad Hall—had in his.

He was supposed to follow my mother on the road, and he did, more or less. But he often turned up at the agreed-upon stopping place somewhat later than planned, having taken a wrong turn here or there. Or here *and* there. He'd drive up to the sad-looking, overheated, waiting group with the smug privileged MG child, and Mother would let him have it. (In the meantime, the rest of us would have had to listen to the warmup. 'Your father! That *man*!') He was apologetic but basically impervious. He could never quite understand what the fuss was about. He'd gotten there, hadn't he? Wasn't that what counted?

At camp, as at home, my mother disappeared into chores—though here they were often shared with her sisters—and into adult pleasures. I can remember her long-limbed slow swim into the deepest water, away from us splashing children. I can remember that she and her sisters liked to sit together and talk over cup after cup of coffee and endless cigarettes, which they took from a seemingly inexhaustible red oval tin of one hundred. Pall Malls. In the evenings they did puzzles together and they talked, a joking, wisecracking kind of talk, full of puns and double entendres, which was too fast, impenetrable to me.

But my father was more available to us here than at home. He still worked every day, of course, scholarly work, usually in one of the smaller cabins. And he too had chores— painting and caulking the rowboats, chopping wood, hauling the foul brimming bucket from the outhouse to the dump. But in the afternoons, he was ours. Patiently and slowly he taught us the skills we needed to negotiate camp independently. How to row a boat. How to hold the canoe paddle, turn it, flutter it. How to do a dead man's float. How to swim. How to pull the cord on the dinky outboard motor, how to make sure you didn't flood it, how to steer the boat away from the hidden underwater rocks that studded our cove. How to cast a fly. How to troll silently. How to reel a fish in, kill it, clean it—what those body parts were, how they functioned. How to tell which mushrooms were poisonous, which you could eat. How to recognize the song of a thrush, of a vireo. Where you were likely to find a lady slipper. How to recognize different varieties of ferns—by size, by texture, by the smell they gave off when you crushed a leaf. How to start a campfire, how to douse it. He'd been an Eagle Scout; I still have his badge. BE PREPARED, it says. And he tried to see that we were, for a kind of life none of us would

74

lead.

But even at home in Chicago it was he who showed us things. In the bitter Chicago winters, he took us on ice skates onto the flooded midway, one after another over the years, guiding us around under his power until we could push off and glide away on our own. He ran alongside the bicycle until we wobbled free down the street. He sat calmly reading in the passenger seat as we learned to drive by tooling around the empty parking lot at the Museum of Science and Industry in the evenings. (Occasionally, if you stalled out or the car lurched too dramatically, he'd lift his head and focus on you for a few minutes, offering a suggestion for improvement, but basically he read.) And because it had been decided I was the artistic one in the family, the musical one (we were each assigned separate strengths, I suppose to keep us from being competitive), he took me with him to performances of music in Rockefeller Chapel, to shows at the Art Institute, and *talked* to me about them afterward—me, a child of eight, or ten, or twelve. About how complicated the tenor's part was, about how much play there was in Picasso's work.

He was patient and respectful—a born teacher, I think, because he was a learner himself, always curious and interested in the world, in other people of any age. I remember how he embarrassed me when he drove me and my friends to dances or parties because of his careful and polite inquisition about what they were studying, what their interests and extracurricular activities were, the colleges they might apply to. God! Why couldn't he just be put-upon and silent, like most parents?

I remember, too, trying to teach him to jitterbug in the back living room. I took the lead, spinning him out, yanking him around to Jerry Lee Lewis, but he was hopeless. Game but hopeless. And in the end, we were laughing too hard to go on anyway.

\*　　　\*　　　\*

And then, when I turned sixteen and went away to college, he vanished from my life suddenly—I can't find him in memory in any sustained way for twenty years or so. I simply stopped knowing him in any real sense.

I think the prime reason initially might have been that, by the unspoken rule in our family—in most families then—my mother was in charge of correspondence, and letters became my connection to home. Actually I tried for a while to enlist my father. I'd become very estranged from my mother from early adolescence on; the mistrust I'd had of her as a little girl had grown into active dislike at this stage. For several years there was nothing she could do that didn't offend me. When she entered a room, I felt compelled to leave it. It was in that mood that I went off to college, with the result that for the first half-year or so I addressed my letters home exclusively to my father or to the family in general, never singling my mother out. Finally my sister wrote to me and asked me to stop, saying it was just too upsetting to my mother, with whom she was still very close. After that, I wrote to them as a unit, and after that it was, of course, only my mother who answered me.

I lived at home for only one more summer after I turned sixteen. I married at twenty, directly after finishing college. By then I'd begun a real rapprochement with my mother, based in some measure, I think, on my wish to see myself as an adult, an equal. But after I had my only child, at twenty-four, I became truly comfortable with her: her love for my baby son was a balm, a healing element to our troubled relationship.

My marriage ended when I was twenty-seven, and I saw more of my parents after that. Occasionally I got to spend time alone with my father, for the most part when we went hiking in the White Mountains near the house they rented in the summers now in New Hampshire, but my mother always dominated our times together. It seemed to me that once her children were grown, she transferred the strong need she had for adult attention—that clear wish to be recognized as the most fascinating, the most charming person in the

77

room—to us. It was now us whom she wished to charm, us whom she wished to seduce. My father had become her competition when we were all together. He was still, of course, her beloved—she never stopped adoring him also—but in this context he was also her rival, her enemy.

I remember one Friday night when I arrived mid-evening at their summerhouse to spend the weekend. I had gotten Ben to bed upstairs, and the three of us, my parents and I, were sitting around in the old wicker furniture, drinking beer and talking for a little while before we went to bed too. My father, unusually enough in this situation, was telling me something—I can't remember what—and I was listening to him attentively when out of the blue, Mother, her voice strident, began to talk too, interrupting him, overriding him, pointing out some peculiarity in the shoes he had on.

We all fell silent, it was so strikingly odd and rude, what she'd done. So desperate. And then he said, 'If I may just complete my sentence,' and continued.

This stands out in my memory because he spoke up for once; he was, if not quite rude himself, at least firm with her. But I remember it also because the whole event seemed to me an apt metaphor for what had happened in my relationship with my father—in my ability to talk to him, to know him: it had been

78

*interrupted.* For years it had been interrupted by my mother's desperation, by her need to be the absolute center of attention.


## CHAPTER FIVE

I am your quintessential WASP—without the family money. Both my parents could trace their roots back through old New England families who left England and Scotland in the seventeenth and eighteenth centuries, the first ones arriving on the *Mayflower*. Gravestones scattered in Massachusetts, Connecticut, Vermont, and Maine bear their ancestors' names: Tappan, Choate, Hastings, Parsons, Winship, Peabodie, Shaw, Noyes. And the wonderful given names are like a calling up of colonial history: Mehitabel, Content, Abiel, Jerusha, Mindwell, Gideon, Mercy, Ephraim, Xenophon, Abigail, Amos. As my father was, so both my grandfathers were ministers; and both their fathers—my great-grandfathers— had been ministers too. On my father's side of the family, the line of clergy goes even more deeply back. So my parents' backgrounds were in almost all ways similar, even down to the large size of their families: four children in my father's, five in my mother's.

Tonally, though, their growing up couldn't have been much more different. My mother's family was intensely female—there'd been four daughters, my mother the oldest, before a son was produced. They were spirited and lively. They liked to laugh. There were endless family stories they all knew and told and retold. There was a party for every occasion and always a crowd to celebrate it. My grandmother was warm and energetic, seemingly imperturbable, and my boisterous grandfather loved any kind of family gathering. At his ninetieth birthday he presided in a yellow T-shirt that read on the front VITA BREVIS? and, on the back, NOT THE REV'S.

But they were competitive too, particularly my mother, the oldest—it almost seemed she needed to assert that no one who'd come after her was quite as important, quite as magnificent, as she was. And they sometimes seemed almost swamped by their memories, as though they enjoyed the past more than they could the present. Nonetheless, we lived more in my mother's family, in their history, their liveliness and jealousies, their ritual gatherings and family ceremonies.

Of course we knew my father's history perfectly well, too. We knew and loved our aunts, his sisters, and the men they married. We visited too with the families on that side and played with those cousins. But the attachments were less charged and therefore in childhood less compelling, the reunions less ritualized and fraught. The comings and goings of my father's side of the family into and out of our lives, and our comings and goings into and out of theirs, simply didn't *count* as much in our childhood. It was my mother's emotional life, after all, that set the tone for us; it was naturally her emotional connection to her family that mattered more.

And my father's family? Well, it was shaped by my grandfather, who was old by the standards of the time when he married: thirty-seven. He was horn in 1874, a Victorian to his bones, so forbidding to his wife's younger sisters that they called him *'Beau-frère'* rather than risk the informality of his first name. He was forty-two when my father was born, and he'd begun to teach church history at Auburn Theological Seminary.

My father's family might have been very different if his mother had lived, but she died young, when he was just eight, and her death marked a change for all of them; afterward there was a chilly quality to their life together.

Two years after my natural grandmother's death, my grandfather remarried. My father, who was incapable of disloyalty, even when it was deserved, was deeply attached to his father and very fond of his stepmother, but my aunts on that side of my family, at least two of whom were devoted to calling a spade a spade, spoke often of a difficult and gloomy growing-up. When the two youngest girls were called back from the home of the beloved aunt they'd been sent to after their mother's death (my father and his older sister stayed home with their father and a housekeeper), they were made to call my grandmother Winifred 'Mother.' They were all discouraged from ever mentioning or remembering aloud their own mother, Marjorie, again.

My grandfather was a patriarch, remote and exacting and almost childishly quick to anger. I have on my mantel a chipped marble bust of Homer that was once his, its nose completely gone and various dings decorating the rest of its head. It's damaged because my grandfather returned home one day to find the maid had *polished* it. He was enraged; one did not *polish* marble! He had a tantrum. He pronounced the bust utterly ruined and took it outside and threw it violently into the ash heap.

My aunts could tell other tales of his temper, of a way he had when irritated of flapping his jowls in frustration or anger. What I remember of my grandfather was the formality of our visits to him late in his life; they were virtually audiences, where we terrified children stood silently to be viewed by an equally silent, unsmiling presence. My father was always careful and respectful to his own father on these occasions.

There is and was a characteristic note sustained in the personalities of my father and his sisters, perhaps genetic but more likely in response to their history. Though all of them were wry, some with sharper wit than others; though all were gracious, curious, interested, and engaged with the world; though all led full and useful lives which brought each of them, I think and hope, enormous satisfaction, there was in all of them a sense, finally, of deep reserve. They were warm but not easily affectionate. Attentive, interested in others, but never demonstrative. I think my father must have been drawn, in part, to the noisiness and energy of my mother and her family. I think, too, that he may have sensed a need for someone like my mother—almost as though he were completing himself by marrying her.

The story of how they met is part of our family's lore. He was getting his doctoral degree at the time. His sister Jane was a classmate of my mother's, and my father had come to Jane's college to visit her. At some point they decided to play tennis. My father hadn't planned for it, and he was unequipped. They found a racket for him to borrow, but he had no appropriate shoes. Where, at a women's college, to find tennis shoes big enough to fit a man?

Ah! Of course! Judy Beach.

The shoes were, in fact, slightly *too* big. My mother was taller than my father, which made her an imposing woman and him an average-sized man. But he was slender and compact and modest, he spoke quietly, he moved in

83

such a contained way that he seemed smaller than he was.

My mother seemed larger. She was long-limbed and wildly expressive. She had long feet too, slender and beautifully arched, with, as far back as I can remember, bright red polish on her toenails in summer. She was excessive in all she did. She spoke in italics, in absolutes: 'I will *never* . . .'; 'a complete and utter *fool*!' She had a loud, gay, genuine laugh, and then too a loud, gay, artificial laugh.

All her life, my father was charmed by her, amused by her, excited by her, and I think occasionally annoyed by her. But he was never, even when she was at her most unreasonable, openly critical of her.

And she could be unreasonable. Sometimes it was funny. One of my uncles told me a story at her memorial service of coming into the primitive kitchen of the camp in Maine early one morning to find Mother alone there in her bathrobe, her face still puffy from sleep or lack of it, drinking coffee, smoking, glowering. She looked at him balefully—he was a cheerful person—and, before he could speak, said, 'Don't you *dare* say good morning to me, Jim Alter!'

Others outside our family also found her wonderfully eccentric and amusing. Several of my cousins told me after her death she was their favorite aunt. One of my father's students said she was the most interesting, the most stimulating, of all the faculty wives.

It was harder to live with her daily, to have her moods be the emotional weather you faced on any given morning. But if there was anyone suited to do it, it was my father. Steady, patient, changeless himself, he rolled with whatever the punch was—though sometimes that detachment, that distance, was the very quality that drove her mad.

Late in his life, but before he was obviously ill, I spent long parts of several summers alone with my father, and he talked to me more than he ever had before about himself. During that time he occasionally expressed regrets to me about this distance. He thought he had hurt my brothers by not being more involved with them as children. He blamed himself for not helping my mother control her drinking, her smoking. But this was a brief period, really, in his long life—only a momentary dwelling in introspection and regret. Very quickly his dispassion, brought on this time by his disease, came to him again. The dying of his brain took away the possibility of some new way of looking at things which he seemed on the verge of finding. And perhaps, after all, this was a variety of kindness.

*       *       *

Some researchers now think that these processes, the processes that caused parts of my father's brain to die slowly, probably begin much earlier than we've realized before in Alzheimer's sufferers. Their work suggests that Dad could have been a victim of the disease for much longer in his life than even the most careful observer might have guessed.

The markers for Alzheimer's disease (AD) are the plaques and neurofibrillary tangles that accumulate in the brain and slowly kill the neurons—the nerve cells—of which the brain is largely composed. These plaques and tangles aren't visible in the living brain through any of the current technologies. It is true that when you scan the Alzheimer's patient's brain for activity, parts of it are blank—wide Seas of Forgetfulness in the fissured, moonlike surface. But this could be caused by any of a number of other diseases or insults to the brain. In fact, until recently, the only way to know definitively that someone has had Alzheimer's disease was retrospectively, posthumously, by autopsy—by looking at the dead brain for those characteristic plaques and tangles.

The tangles—neurofibrillary tangles, or NFTs in the literature—are altered neuronal elements: actually formerly part of the brain but changed both in structural appearance and chemical nature. The plaques—senile plaques, or SPs—are extracellular deposits of aggregated proteins, an abnormal and complex material, waxy and translucent, primarily composed of beta-amyloid. Normally the protein is benign and soluble. In the course of Alzheimer's disease there is an increase in its amount and also a change in its form, so that it becomes fibrous and toxic to neurons.

When you look at microscopic pictures of these plaques and tangles, stained, there's a Jackson Pollock quality to their appearance. The tangles appear the darker of the two, like small distinct blobs of paint thrown hard at the canvas—so hard that often a thin tail is left streaking out behind. The plaques are bigger, more amorphous blobs than the tangles, with less-well-defined edges.

There are smaller dark squiggles visible under the microscope too, called, in this world, 'curly fibers.' They are threads made of swollen synaptic nerve fibers—nerve endings normally involved in the passage of electrical impulses—which have now become fibrillar: fibrous. In the house I grew up in there was a linoleum on the kitchen floor that, though more riotous in color than any of the available stains used to reveal these structures, bore some resemblance in its splattered pattern to this picture of disease.

The combined effect of the growth of these amyloid deposits and the transformation of normal brain cells into neurofibrillary tangles is simply to stop brain activity in the damaged areas. Where those blobs and tangles occur, signals fizzle out in the brain, unable to pass through the fibrous thicket, the unresponsive plaque. Events that occur and are seen cannot 'get across' to be apprehended, to be recorded in memory. Signals from the body—a full bladder, hunger—are no longer able to trigger the socially appropriate response—or any other response. Things that are seen cannot be recognized or categorized correctly.

The typical age of perceptible onset is sometime in the victim's seventies, but it can be much earlier; and the fact is that neurofibrillary tangles have been found in brains as young as twenty, long before symptoms are in evidence. It seems possible, then, that Alzheimer's is a lifelong disease whose expression in dementia is simply the closing episode, a kind of crossing the threshold for the long-failing brain, the last step that finally makes clear what the earlier steps have meant.

A few years ago there was a highly speculative research project done using writing samples collected early in life from nuns whose histories through old age and death were known and whose lives, because they were all in the same convent, were presumably controlled after the age of twenty or so for many variables. The nuns whose writing samples were more elemental—whose thinking, as expressed in the writing, was more reductive—had a very high incidence of later mental impairment or posthumously diagnosed Alzheimer's disease. But both 'high idea density' and greater grammatical complexity were consistently characteristic of the writing samples of nuns at age twenty-two who would still be mentally intact fifty-eight years later.

One of the possible implications of this study seems to be that we may gradually learn to recognize other markers of the disease earlier than the now-familiar dementia; that there will be aspects of the personality or behaviors we think of now as completely normal that we will come to understand as connected to the illness and symptomatic of it.

After I read this article, I spent a few days looking back at my father's younger self and wondering whether some aspects of his personality that seemed so essentially *who he was* might really have been the disease expressing itself. Or, alternatively, whether the disease was so entwined with who he was, even early on, as to be part of him. Perhaps it could account for his even temperament, I thought, his imperviousness to mayhem, noise. Even some of what gave him sex appeal to my mother might have been connected to it—his abstractedness, his distractedness, which she saw as evidence of his intellectual superiority, his fineness as a person.

I thought too about the dynamics between them, and what their deeper meaning might be if he had the disease much earlier than we thought. Because it was in my mother's nature to try to absorb other people, to yearn for a kind of merging with those she loved intensely. All her life she threw herself against what she saw as the mystery of my father, the self he was hiding from her. His unavailability to her kept her pursuing him, sometimes desperately, sometimes angrily, sometimes adoringly. Perhaps then it was in part his Alzheimer's-ness she fell in love with. Perhaps what she was really engaged with in her lifelong struggle was his disease. And perhaps, then, her struggle kept him attached to life, working to resist his illness, to keep certain synapses firing longer than they might have otherwise. There are, in the brain, chemical substances called neurotransmitters that open channels between nerve cells, allowing for the possibilities of what are called 'action potentials,' the passing of impulses between the cells—the source of all thought and behavior. One of these neurotransmitters, serotonin, has been made famous by Prozac. Another one, which is notably diminished in the brains of people with Alzheimer's disease, is acetylcholine. This diminishment is thought to be partly responsible for the diminished brain activity of Alzheimer's patients. In fact, several of the few therapies used now for Alzheimer's patients are based in finding ways to increase or replace lost acetylcholine.

It's funny to me to think of my mother as a

chemical force in this sense, laying siege to my father's brain, insisting, 'Fire, damn you! Fire!' And perhaps even having some success: the structures of the brain are changing constantly in response to the use of sensory pathways. We *can* affect the microscopic shape of our brains with what we study, what we learn, what we do. The brain of a musician is different from the brain of a quarterback, in part because they have repeatedly stimulated quite different pathways in quite different ways. When my mother wailed to my father, 'I would like you *just once, just once* to try and remember what it was that attracted you to me in the first place!' maybe she was really insisting that he lay down some new neural pathways, just for her. And if he did it, and did it often enough, maybe that added density helped him resist AD a little longer than he might have otherwise.

My mother may have made a kind of invisible dent in my father after all.

\*       \*       \*

There are researchers, though, who believe we are all pre-Alzheimer's. They point to the occurrence of plaques and tangles in the brains of normal, sane older people as evidence for this. Of course, in the nonsymptomatic brain they are smaller in number and more confined; but if these people lived long enough, the theory goes—and maybe some of them would have to live 120, 130, or 140 years—their brains too would gradually be destroyed by these same processes. *When* you get the disease, *how fast* it progresses: these are a matter of luck—or of certain risk factors. But these researchers believe that the increase in the percentage of people with Alzheimer's as you look at each decade of old age is just the beginning of a steady line on a chart that would rise inevitably to 100 percent if we prolonged life more or less indefinitely—if we 'saved' people from all the other ways of dying.

In this context, what sense can be made of the differences drawn among the nuns' writing samples? Or of my notion that perhaps I could have been seeing the disease in my father at age forty, or forty-five, or fifty?

There will be answers to some of the questions and conflicts raised by these theories in years to come—and to many others. Nearly every day now there is new information about the disease and about the brain generally. The development of extraordinary new technologies for looking at what goes on in the living brains of normal people as well as in those with organic brain diseases like schizophrenia has already explained a great deal about what the physiological bases are for various behaviors and for various 'misunderstandings' of the universe: hallucinations, delusions. Other research will lead to a clearer explanation of what causes illnesses such as Alzheimer's disease. For now we can say that the specific history of each Alzheimer's patient—when he or she fails and at what offers a unique map, if we care to draw it, of what is happening in that patient's brain, where it is happening, and how fast cells are dying.

*     *     *

Phrenology is a curious theory, curious in some measure because it anticipated crudely the truth that specialized parts of the brain control, in connection with other parts, specific aspects of human thought and behavior. Phrenology erred in seeing each of these areas, or centers, as utterly independent of the others and as reflecting certain isolable human *traits*: intelligence, 'amativeness,' wit, conscientiousness, and so on. Proponents of phrenology also believed, erroneously, that the more highly developed a faculty was, the larger the center of that faculty in the head would be—skull included. Thus you could understand something about a person by running your hand over his head, recording with your fingertips those enlarged areas on the skull— the phrenological 'bumps.'

Now surely not many people took all of this as factually, literally true. But these ideas, like those of psychiatry, achieved a kind of currency anyway in the culture at large, became part of the general vocabulary, part of the way you could think about what made people as they were. We can see them emerge in nineteenth-century literature, just as ideas based on Freudian psychology have in twentieth-century literature. Here is Poe's description of the uselessly brilliant, neurasthenic Roderick Usher.

A cadaverousness of complexion; an eye large, liquid, and luminous beyond comparison; lips somewhat thin and very pallid, but of a surpassingly beautiful curve; a nose of a delicate Hebrew model, but with a breadth of nostril unusual in similar formations; a finely moulded chin, speaking, in its want of prominence, of a want of moral energy . . . these features, with an inordinate expansion above the regions of the temple, made up altogether a countenance not easily to be forgotten.

My father, too, had a high forehead and an open intellectual liveliness in his face until AD clouded his eyes and slackened his mouth. If I were a phrenologist, I might have theorized that he was governed by intelligence, specifically *causality, comparison, eventuality, time.* All these occur in the forehead and temples, so pronounced and well shaped in my father.

94

But new research tells us that even in the beetle-browed it isn't the size of the skull, much less of the brain or any part of the brain, that matters. Rather it's the speed, the efficiency, and the density of neural pathways, those developed networks of connections between nerve cells in the brain. It may be for this reason that low education levels are a risk factor for AD—because education increases the density of neural pathways—'works' the brain, as it were. And at least one theory proposes that with equal numbers of tangles and plaques, the educated brain simply has more alternative options left for neuronal firing than the uneducated one—more ways for thought processes still to take place. 'Neurocognitive reserve,' it's called. Take twenty pathways away, and the educated person still has another twenty, carefully developed by reading, by study, by making the brain perform certain tasks.

This may be, too, why smoking has been seen in some studies as a *negative* risk factor: nicotine activates acetylcholine receptors in the brain and thus indirectly facilitates and speeds the passing of impulses between nerve cells.

There are risk factors and negative risk factors. There's a genetic component to at least some forms of the disease. And the threshold for its appearance symptomatically may vary with different histories, different brains, different lives, different ages. But when enough of the neurons that compose the critical pathways slow down in their activity, shrink, or die, then even the person with the most elegant brow, with the highest level of education, with the most acetylcholine zinging around in his brain experiences changes in his behavior. And in these changes in behavior, the amazing specificity of the parts of the brain reveals itself.

My father never lost the ability to recall the names of those who had been important to him or to remember in some essential way who they were. Well after he'd been diagnosed, I took him to a picnic in the summer town we went to in New Hampshire, and his dear friend Peggy Grant came up to shake his hand, telling him her name as she did so. He commented on it afterward, wondering why she'd done that—because he didn't need her kind reminder. We'd spoken of Peggy often, and he had mentioned looking forward to seeing her that day. Similarly I could name his nieces and nephews, his colleagues from Princeton or the University of Chicago, his friends, my siblings, his grandchildren—and he knew, he always knew us all.

He had trouble, though, with new names. He called the woman who came in to help him get dressed and shaved and ready to greet the day by a variety of names: Alice, Arlette, or sometimes Jonathan or 'that boy'—wrong category, Dad. Her name was Marlene, and he was very fond of her, but there was no way for him to retain this little fact.

Why should this have been?

It happened because the part of his brain whose function was to transfer new information into memory, the hippocampus, was being destroyed by Alzheimer's disease. New names, new skills—how to open the door on *my* car, for instance, or how to work the remote controls for a television—these couldn't be retained for more than a few days because they couldn't get past the hippocampus into permanent 'storage' in other parts of the brain.

He began to have trouble, too, with ordinary nouns, and his speech became more and more riddled with substitutions. And of course it turns out there's a place in the brain specific to nouns, to naming things. Typically, when this region is damaged, the person sounds much the same, his rhythms of speech are intact, but he uses pronouns instead of nouns, and generic words or categories instead of instances. When my brother and his son and his son's beautiful Latina fiancée visited Dad one day, he remembered the visit to report to me and he remembered them, but he said Bob and Marc had come to call with 'a Chinese man.'

Sometimes he'd substitute the name of part of something for the whole. I remember my confusion when he was trying to tell me something was wrong with his rocking chair, because he kept calling it 'the cloth' or 'the weaving.' When he finally retrieved the color correctly—'the green weaving'—I suddenly recognized that the reference was to his old Victorian rocker with the worn green velvet cover.

Categories and names of relationships flummoxed him. When a polite, mentally intact resident asked, 'Oh, is this your daughter?' he answered, 'No, I'm his . . . mother.'

Still, he had my name. He could remember my mother by her name. And he could remember her—not always whether she was dead or alive, but *her*—her being, her essence. Stories about her, or about others who had been dear to him, could still light his face and make him laugh. I took pride in this. 'He never didn't know me,' I say now when people say it must have been terrible. And that is almost true. There were seconds or minutes one time when he seemed not to know who I was, but he always greeted me warmly when I first arrived; he always understood, in the first flood of pleasure, our relation to each other. I knew other people whose parent or spouse had lost this part of memory nearer the beginning of the illness. I knew how painful, how isolating that was, and my gratitude that this part of his brain was left to Dad—to all of us—was deep.

*     *     *

The visual pathways in his brain began to fail. The first thing to go had been his ability to read, to connect those symbols on the page with a meaning—though he could still pick out words separately, evidence that the problem was not purely with his eyesight. Still, it was his eyesight he blamed, and it was with his eyesight that he wanted help. He had had cataracts removed while he was in Denver, and in fact one cornea had by now clouded a little again, so I took him to the eye doctor for that; we drove to the hospital in Concord one day and I watched as Dad sat forward in the darkened room, his chin resting on a stabilizer, and the laser quickly, magically, cleared that eye again.

But it didn't give him back what he had imagined it would—his ability to read and, beyond that, probably, some old sense of himself. He went on asking me, each time I visited, to take him for another appointment to the eye doctor, to get him a new prescription, a new pair of glasses, and I continued to put him off. As time went by he grew irritated at my slowness to respond to his need, at my indifference, as he must have seen it, to his dilemma.

And so finally, unable to bear that, I scheduled another appointment. I asked the doctor ahead of time to try to help my father understand that new glasses wouldn't help. And because he was a doctor, because he was a man, my father listened to him, and for a few days remembered: *There was something organically wrong, but it wasn't with his eyes, it was with the messages between his eyes and his brain.* And then he forgot and began to agitate again for another doctor's appointment.

Increasingly now, too, he misunderstood—'misread'—the visual. Oliver Sacks has written about our way of seeing as being learned; and scientists have begun to understand that, if certain visual synapses—electrical connections between nerve cells in the various visual systems of the brain—aren't formed and 'exercised,' built up, by a certain age, they can't be developed later. Sacks speaks of a blind patient whose sight was given to him surgically in middle age who never learned 'how' to see certain things.

And now I watched my father as those synapses stopped working in his brain, as he 'unlearned' seeing. Shadows became for him not the absence of light but dark *objects*, as perhaps they appear to infants and little children. Their presence was inexplicable and disturbing to him. His own shadow underfoot on a sunny day, for instance, was often an irritant, a strange black animal dogging him. He would sometimes kick or swat at it as we walked along.

In the later stages of his illness, he stopped 'seeing' food on the left side of his plate. At first everyone worried about his appetite, because he was growing so thin anyway. But then an attendant noticed the pattern. He was pleased and excited to report to me that if he simply rotated Dad's plate a half circle, he'd soldier on and clear off the whole thing.

Some 'hallucinations' may have been simply mistakes. I thought for a while that his seeing a bull in the yard outside his window was hallucinatory until I noticed in the Victorian iron bench out there two curving back pieces like horns and, below those, a pair of floral motifs that looked like eyes. Just a misreading of what was there, then, not purely an invention.

Sometimes it wasn't clear what was going on. One day, as we were leaving his room, he gestured at his bathrobe, hanging from a hook. 'Dave Swift,' he said, and laughed. 'He's been standing there all day.' And I looked at the bathrobe, hung there like a tall, skinny man in plaid, skinnier than my Uncle Dave but not by all that much, and I laughed too. But thinking about it later, I couldn't figure out whether this was a mistake or a joke, a misreading or a hallucination. Who could say what was going on in what part of the brain?

And what were the impediments he saw late in his illness that caused him to tiptoe so carefully over something I couldn't see, or to get down on the floor and crawl around it? Simple disturbances in his visual pathways, in the way he saw something *real*? or internally elicited disturbances that led him to invent something where there was nothing—to hallucinate?

Of course, he had delusions too. When we were visiting one day, he told my husband that there was an underground railroad at Sutton Hill. My husband laughed, thinking that Dad was making a joke about his wish to escape. But later in the day Dad soberly pointed out to him the spot where the train pulled in. And Marlene reported to me that she found him at this spot more than once, that he told her he was waiting for the train.

Oddly, this seems not unconnected to the intention of the design of Sutton Hill. The shops and the bank, post office, and grocery store were all arrayed along what was called Main Street, an indoor walkway with an old-fashioned clock tower at one end. All had whimsical storefronts. Why not give Main Street a railroad station in your imagination too?

Sometimes the delusions were painful, like the one about my sister being abducted by terrorists. I tried to reassure him that time; I reported that I'd spoken to her and she was safe in Denver. But he couldn't be comforted. He persisted. He found me, I think, hard-hearted in the face of his certainty that she was in mortal danger. Finally I called my sister to ask her to get in touch with him herself and tell him she was all right.

Sometimes the delusions were pleasant. He told me about wild, elaborate gatherings with other residents. They were putting on a play together. They'd had a kind of combined lawn and pajama party. Sometimes he would have heard an old friend, often someone long dead, lecture or preach. Sometimes he'd see Mother. I came to feel that these were the residue of dreams, dreams that seemed no less real to him than the fractured reality he had to live through each day and so, in his interpretation, became a part of that reality.

Not all Alzheimer's patients have hallucinations and delusions; the estimates vary wildly in the literature from 30 to 60 or 70 percent. For those who don't, the course of the disease is simply progressive cognitive deterioration. But when they are present, they too are traceable to conditions in quite specific parts of the brain and probably also to failures within networks linking certain areas.

Hallucinations and delusions in AD patients are born in the same areas of the brain in which schizophrenics are also disturbed—primarily those areas responsible for receiving visual and auditory signals. But the nature of the Alzheimer's hallucinations and delusions is generally different from those of the schizophrenic. More often, schizophrenics see themselves at the center of the delusion. *They* are being persecuted, *they* are being abducted by terrorists or monitored by the CIA. In any case, they are the main actors in the drama. The Alzheimer's patient is more likely to stand to the side, as Dad did at this stage of his delusions. More likely to report that others around him are doing bizarre things or that someone else is in trouble or danger. More often he has been just a witness, as we so often are in dream life, to the strange misadventures and tragedies around him.

And oddly, though the presence of hallucinations and delusions is correlated with a more rapidly advancing version of Alzheimer's and some researchers are inclined therefore to see it as a subset of AD, most experts believe that there is *less* cortical damage, *less* ventricular enlargement, in the hallucinating or delusional patient at this stage of the disease. It is as though the patient *needs* more cortex to develop and elaborate the hallucinatory or delusional ideas.

I knew neither of those facts at the time. I'm grateful, of course, not to have known the first, that these symptoms are associated with a quicker arrival at what is euphemistically called the 'cognitive end point' of the disease. But if I'd known the second fact—that these symptoms may indicate more cortex—I'm sure I would have taken pride in it. *Why is he so crazy? Ha! Because he's got more brain left.*

This is how we are, after all, watching the people we love disappear. This is what is left to us; this is the comfort we can take. 'He was never violent.' 'She always loved being with the children.' 'She's just as stubborn as ever.' I took pride in my father's always recognizing me, as I was proud that he retained his graciousness, that he always said to Marlene— and, later, his other caretaker, Nancy—'It was grand to see you' when he'd run into them in the hallways. I was even proud when he had an elaborate delusion about the Civil War near the end of his life and mistook my foot for Antietam. *Who but Dad?* I thought. *Who but Dad?*

Whatever the remotely personal characteristic that seems to have escaped the disease, we seize on it. Whatever idiosyncratic neuronal patterns still fire, still express something laid down with care and attention and love years earlier—this is important, and we cling to it. *He's not just an Alzheimer's victim. He's still, somehow, himself. He's managed to hold on, to outwit this disease, in this one or two or three ways.*

But of course, I knew better. Outwitting the disease isn't possible. It wasn't owing to his character or depth of attachment to people that Dad remembered us. It was what the disease spared while it destroyed something else. He could have stopped recognizing us earlier and forgone the delusions. He could

105

have dropped verbs—there is a part of the brain specific to verbs—and been stuck with a list of nouns to repeat without much skill at connecting them by actions. It was the *disease* that determined what would go first and what would be left, not vice versa.

I remember talking about him with an old friend of mine, someone who'd known Dad too, years before. By then, near his death, Dad was occasionally violent, and I recounted that to this friend.

He shook his head. 'Isn't it strange,' he said, 'that under that gentle, sweet exterior there should be all that violence?'

A different model, this one: Freudian. One that saw the constraint of the superego eaten away by the disease, and the elemental core, the uncontrolled center, the id, as still remaining, unbuffered. The violent Dad who was secretly always there, emerging now that he'd lost control of himself.

No, I said. No, that's not the way it worked. It was his *brain*, not a theoretical construct in his *mind*, that was being destroyed. He was *organically* a different person. I was trying to be pleasant and conversational, but I remember feeling a real anger, even a contempt, for my friend in his misunderstanding.

Yet I indulged myself—didn't I?—in the correlate belief: that the good stuff he retained, he retained because of who he was:

106

because of the fineness, the excellence, of who he was. And that was just as much a superstition, a fiction, but one I didn't wish to shake. And I didn't ask myself to shake it, though I did know it was a fiction. 'He never didn't know me,' I said proudly. 'Up to the end, he knew me.'

Technically, importantly, this was true. But there were several times when his gaze at me went blank, momentarily, though he'd known who I was seconds before. And one of the times he was violent with me, when I was struggling physically with him to bring him inside after a walk and he didn't want to come—the last outside walk we took—he looked at me with hatred and contempt and I think he didn't know me at all. I hope not, actually. I hope he did think I was someone else.

But even the last time I visited him when he was conscious, he recognized me at first.

When I came into his room, he was standing by his crib bed, gripping its rails with white-knuckled intensity and staring fixedly at something he was seeing on his blanket. He was slightly bent at this point, a gentle Parkinsonian curve to his back. I spoke to him, but he didn't seem to hear me. I went over and touched him, I swung my head just under his face and looked up at him, smiling.

'Hi, Dad,' I said.

He started. 'Why, Susie!' he said, calling me

by my little-girl name. And it seemed that he was actually *seeing* me as a little girl in that moment, his smile was so delighted, his voice so light and glad.

He knew me. I clung to that, to those happy moments at the start of each visit—before I denied what he knew to be true. Before I failed to respond humanely to what he reported as calamity. Before I told him what I could not or would not do for him today—take him to the doctor, find his books, get his car back. Before he said, as he did at least every other time I got up to leave, 'Say . . . are you driving? I was wondering if, maybe, you could give me a lift home.'

## CHAPTER SIX

Listen sometime to the way people speak of others' deaths, of their dying. It's full of judgment—censure here, praise there. What we all approve of, what we like in a death, is the dignified old person, still relatively intact physically and all there mentally, who carefully puts his clothes away one night, goes to bed, and never wakes up. We like someone who doesn't suffer terribly and make us watch that suffering. *Who has all his marbles* till the day he goes, who *just doesn't get up one day.* 'That's the way to do it,' we say, as though praising a canny decision.

Susan Sontag, in *Illness as Metaphor*, writes about the phenomenon of blaming people for their illnesses:

> With the modern diseases (once TB, now cancer), the romantic idea that the disease expresses the character is invariably extended to assert that the character causes the disease—because it has not expressed itself. Passion moves inward, striking and blighting the deepest cellular recesses . . . Such preposterous and dangerous views manage to put the onus of the disease on the patient.

I felt this kind of judgment on Dad in his fellow residents at Sutton Hill. He always lived among the general population there (no such thing as an Alzheimer's ward yet, just that short time ago!) and I could sense their recoiling from him. Annie, one of his nurses, funny and loving but indiscreet to the core, confirmed it for me—the irritation and contempt his neighbors felt for him. 'Those old ladies,' she said, shaking her head, full of her own judgment. 'They act like you get to *choose* the way you go.'

I was sorry Annie told me this, but I wasn't surprised. The fact was, of course, that I recognized my own judgments in theirs. I even recognized Dad's judgments. I remembered he'd said, years earlier, of the wife of an old acquaintance who had Alzheimer's disease, 'I hear she's completely ga-ga now.' The tone was mocking, not kind—surely the same kind of thing, in the same kind of voice, that his neighbors said about him now. That I had said about wacky old people, too, and felt about them. Until my own father turned wacky.

I think, until I lived through my father's dying, that I thought death finished a person's story, that it was part of the narrative arc of someone's life and made a kind of final sense of it. The deaths I'd known until then—and there hadn't been many, my family was so long-lived—had misled me in this regard. I thought you *earned* a certain kind of death. That my grandparents were still alive and wholly themselves because of *who they were* somehow; because of how they'd lived. And my mother! Well, hadn't she had the very death she would have wished? In an evening dress, at a party, drinking, smoking, after a day of pleasure and deep, satisfying excitement?

*       *       *

In 1979, my mother was sixty years old, two years older than I am as I write this. She was full of intellectual curiosity, full of energy and life, full of ego and emotion, full of herself. My father had a sabbatical that year, starting in the fall, which coincided with his retirement as

110

academic dean from Princeton Theological Seminary, where he'd gone when he left the University of Chicago—from now on he would just teach church history. My parents decided they'd rent their house out and come to live in Cambridge, near me, for that semester.

I had mixed feelings about this, feelings that centered, of course, on her. Would she drop by constantly? Would she want to see me all the time? More accurately, *Would she eat me alive?!* I was especially worried because 1979 marked a time of change for me in my writing life, and I was afraid her needs would somehow interrupt that life.

I had begun, only a year or so before, to send stories out, first to magazines that might pay me something, then to little literary magazines. Nothing had been accepted, but I'd had what writers call 'good' rejection letters, personally written ones; and I had an odd kind of confidence in myself, an assumption that it would happen—my work getting taken for publication—and it would happen soon. I'd begun to meet other writers through a few classes I'd taken, and then among the parents in the day-care center where I worked. The winter before, I'd applied to graduate writing programs—not so much for the sake of the course work as because I thought I might get a fellowship that would let me stop working and write more or less full time for a while.

I did get a fellowship—several fellowships,

actually. I could choose where I wanted to go. The biggest dollar amount, though, was from Boston University's Creative Writing program, the program that would also be the least disruptive to my life. I could stay home. More important, Ben could stay home. There would be no complicated moves and adjustments to make. I accepted BU's offer and was looking forward to living and working in a community of writers for a year. What I feared was that my parents' arrival might threaten that in some way. Nonetheless, I found them a big lovely house to rent about five blocks away from mine.

On the evening they arrived down from their summerhouse in New Hampshire, they came first to me. Mother was tearful and tired, overwhelmed—unreasonably, it seemed to me—by the thought of the cat they were going to have to care for: it came with the house, and she foresaw difficulties because of their old dog, who came with *them.*

Already! I thought, irritated with her.

I drove up with them to show them the rental. We entered through the back door, into the big kitchen. There, on the table, was a note from the friend of the owner who was in charge of the house while the owner was gone.

Groans from Mother: Oh, God, what on *earth* was this about? She started to read it out loud to us.

The friend welcomed us. She told us where

112

things were, who to contact in case of various kinds of emergencies, how to reach her. Then she said that she was sorry to have to tell us that, tragically, the cat had recently died. Mother whooped with mean joy and literally danced around the kitchen. Dad and I couldn't help laughing with her. By the time I left she'd poured herself a stiff drink and was happily taking in the big open rooms they would live in for four months.

Nothing happened that fall as I'd feared it could. It was as though the convenient and welcome death of the cat were a kind of perverse blessing. My mother, who had begun to write poetry again after years away from it, enrolled in a class at the Radcliffe Seminars and was almost as busy as I was. My father went daily to the Divinity School Library at Harvard. I saw them only two or three times a week, sometimes for a meal, sometimes for a shorter visit. They poked around Boston and Cambridge together, and I think Mother felt, in a way, returned to her youth; her father had had a church in Belmont when she was an adolescent. They took care of Ben, who was then eleven, on the day he had no school in the afternoon, which was one of my longest days on campus at BU. It was an easy, lovely time for us all. I remember that my father came over one day and helped me plant a dogwood in my front yard. They both came over for Thanksgiving—Ben was with his father—and between courses, my father and I raked and bagged the fallen maple leaves in my tiny backyard while Mother sat wrapped up on the deck in the slanted gold afternoon sun, drinking wine and crying out from time to time about how *divine* this was.

I gathered, though, that my father's work wasn't going very well. My mother confided to me that being a dean for fifteen years had 'absolutely *ruined* your father as a scholar.' I wasn't sure how to take this—whether it was just part of the usual drama she always tended toward, or of the jealousy she'd always felt about the extra demands being dean put on my father and about the freedom the president of the seminary had felt to call on Dad at virtually any time.

But he complained, too, of not getting much done. He had a grant during this sabbatical to work on a revision of his biggest text, *The History of Christianity, 1650–1950*, and he clearly felt his usual strong sense of obligation to accomplish a lot on that account. But he also saw the text as embarrassingly hostile to Catholicism, something that seemed particularly egregious in these post-Ecumenical Council years. He wanted very much to change it, because the world of the church itself had changed and he along with it. It was odd, then, and probably more distressing to him than he said, that he was off his stride somehow with his scholarly work.

My mother, on the other hand, was working very hard at her poetry and was unusually happy—except for her own beloved mother's sudden illness, a stroke, which had kept my mother driving frequently to New Haven from mid-fall on to see her. By Thanksgiving, though, it seemed clear my grandmother would survive and recover completely, and my mother was ready to turn to her end-of-the-semester paper on Elizabeth Bishop with enthusiasm.

The ten days or so after our Thanksgiving meal together were busy for me too. I had several term papers and also some fiction to write. My son went off to stay at his father's house for a week, and I holed up with my typewriter and a lot of take-out food and didn't see my parents until December eighth, the day after I turned my last paper in.

That morning was unusually warm and sunny for December. I picked my mother up at about ten and we went Christmas shopping together, hitting one funky Cambridge store after another. She loved the shops, so different from those in Princeton. She was cheerful and exuberant. At Mobilia they were serving mulled wine. 'Why, certainly!' my mother said, and she had two glasses full as we looked at things.

Later in the day, she called me to tell me that my younger brother's first child, a boy to be named Michael, had just been born by

115

cesarean section. I stood in the kitchen, listening to the italics in her voice. She sounded high, exultant. Oh! she had to rush off now, she said. She and Dad were going out to tea in Belmont at my great-aunt's house. Later I found out that Mother got into an intense political argument there—she enjoyed nothing more. That evening, I knew, they were to go to a dinner party in Cambridge.

I was alone that night, finally with time to work on Christmas presents. When I'd finished sewing a few things, I took advantage of my son's absence to go to bed early and read. I had turned the light out, but wasn't asleep, when the phone rang around midnight. It was my father. He apologized for waking me. My mother, he said, had collapsed at dinner and been taken to the hospital with an apparent heart attack.

*'And?'* I said. 'How is she?'

He cleared his throat. 'She's gone.'

I cried out, 'No!' (My tenant, a dear friend through all these years, says she remembers that night, remembers the wild cry she heard through the walls and only later learned the cause of.) After a moment, I was able to ask a few questions. And then suddenly it seemed crazy to be talking on the phone. Here we were, only a few blocks apart. I had to be with my father. I had to go. I got dressed and drove up Avon Hill, and we sat in the rented kitchen, dry-eyed and stunned, until around four-thirty

116

or five in the morning, both of us—as we said again and again—fully expecting my mother to waltz in at any moment and begin *pronouncing* on one thing or another.

I think this feeling was compounded for him because he hadn't seen her again after her collapse at the party. She'd been wearing her evening dress, talking and drinking, and then suddenly she sat down, yawned once or twice, and slumped over, unconscious. When the ambulance came, the EMT guys asked my father about her medications. He wasn't sure of all of them, so he drove home to gather them up instead of going in the ambulance with Mother.

By the time he got back to the hospital with her collection of pill bottles, she was dead, though he didn't know it right away. He sat in the waiting room as they continued to work on her for a while. When they came to tell him their news, he asked to see her, but they discouraged him; they told him what they'd done to try to save her had been invasive and might be difficult for him to confront. He acceded to them, as was his nature. (And indeed, when we picked up her rings and clothing a few days later, there was blood—Mother's dried brown blood—on everything.)

But I think now that not seeing her dying, or dead, made it hard for him to accept completely what had happened. That, and her dramatic and bottomless vitality. One moment

117

she was herself, theatrical and full of vivid life; then she was gone from the stage, disappeared forever. No wonder in his delusional life a few years later she was often there, alive and busy with one thing or another.

\*    \*    \*

Over the next few days we planned a service and made the arrangements. My siblings and their families assembled slowly, my poor younger brother leaving his wife and day-old son in a hospital in Colorado to come east and mourn his mother. The rented house was noisy, full of the exuberance of the young kids, almost all boys.

The doorbell rang one morning in the midst of this. I answered it. It was the director of the funeral home who'd arranged for Mother's cremation. He'd come to drop off her ashes. I took the box. It was glossy cardboard, square and white, like the boxes that held the corsages boys gave you in high school. I remember standing with it in the wide front hall after I'd closed the door, listening to the happy shrieks of my nephews and my son playing wildly, unsure what to do. My father was upstairs in his room with the door shut, which seemed to be the way he was managing his grief. I didn't know whether it would be an intrusion to knock on the door and give him the box. I couldn't even decide on an appropriate place

118

to set the box down if I didn't take it upstairs. I don't remember, actually, what I did do with it—but I remember feeling overwhelmed, suddenly, one of many moments through those days when I felt as though the simplest choices were beyond me.

We had the service in New Haven, near where my grandparents, then in their mid-eighties, lived and a location central to many in Mother's vast family. Each of us, my grandfather included, rose and went up to the pulpit to speak or read something in the service. My father had the 23rd Psalm. I read a poem of Mother's.

The day was long. We had arranged a lunch for the whole extended family at a local hotel. I was sitting two seats down from my grandfather at the long table. I remember that at one point he reached over and pushed the full plate away from the person sitting between us as he spoke to him, as though this poor man's lunch might distract him—and surely he wouldn't want that!—from what my grandfather was saying. I remember thinking how like him my mother had been in her hunger for attention and admiration.

After lunch we stopped at my grandparents' retirement condo to visit my grandmother, still recovering from her stroke and unable to come to the service. Then there was the long dark drive back to Boston. The next day, my brothers and sister left and Dad's rental house seemed suddenly vast and silent. We began to clean it, and he, slowly, to pack things up.

*  *  *

My father couldn't go back to New Jersey until February; my parents had rented their house out for the entire semester. They had taken the Cambridge house only until just after the New Year, having planned to travel together for the remaining time. This was something he couldn't imagine doing now, alone. Instead, just before Christmas he moved in with me for a month.

His possessions sat for those weeks in boxes and suitcases heaped against the wall in the kitchen. It was only on the second or third day that I noticed the white corsage-sized box that held Mother's ashes in the pile, as though it were of no more importance than the books or clothes. For my own ease of mind I tucked it away below other things, so my father's dog or my cat or the kids running in and out wouldn't bump into it and knock it to the floor, but it startled me as a fact about Dad that he would treat the ashes so casually.

I needed to explain it to myself, and the way I did this was to attribute it to his complete lack of sentimentality: for him, I concluded, no part of Mother was contained or represented by the ashes, by the idea of the ashes, by the presence of the white box. Wherever her memory, her soul, dwelt for him, it wasn't there.

Was I right? I don't know. Maybe, I think now, he was already a little Alzheimer-y, flattened in his response to some things, as in his apparent forgetfulness of the meaning of the box. Maybe another, intact version of Dad would have been more careful, more . . . reverential somehow about it. But maybe not.

We tried to live a normal life. On New Year's Eve we went to a Scandinavian friend's house for a splendid dinner, and in accordance with Norwegian custom we stood on our chairs and jumped down from them as the New Year commenced, signaling our new beginnings.

We drove out to Lincoln one night to have dinner with my aunt and uncle, my mother's youngest sister and her husband. Dad's birthday was January 11. He was sixty-five, officially elderly, as I told him (as I was now, at thirty-five, officially middle-aged). I cooked a fancy dinner and made a cake, and he blew out the candles. Ben was there, and a cousin had stopped by for the night, so it felt, I thought, festive. Festive enough.

We went to movies; we took Ben and friends out for hamburgers; we stayed busy. But there was often a slight sense of strain, the awareness of silence, of the absence of the person who would have been decrying something, exalting something—even tediously describing something—but occupying center stage, at any rate, and thereby letting the two of us off the social hook. We missed her. My father usually had one drink before dinner, and I took to having one—and often several others—with him. It made things easier for both of us.

Over these weeks my father's behavior made me hopeful that he would approach his new solitary life with the discipline and curiosity that had marked him in all his endeavors: a new subject to study, a new sad project to begin. It seemed this might he so; he had a note pad, and he followed me around the house, asking questions and writing down the bits of useful information he was gathering. 'About how often do you vacuum?' he'd ask, and write down my answer. (My answer! I hope I gave him the *theoretical* number.) 'How often do you clean the toilets?' Scribble, scribble. He listed household products I used and asked and noted *how* I used them.

I had to show him how to balance a checkbook—astonishing to me, and then not: of course she'd kept the accounts. She'd run the whole show. Everything to free him to be purely, only, the brilliant scholar she felt him to be.

I discovered, going over their books, that they had no money to speak of, that when they'd loaned me $5,000 for the bulk of the down payment on my house, when they'd loaned my siblings money for their houses as well, they were cleaning themselves out each time, giving us everything they had, in checking as well as savings. I think none of us would have guessed this or perhaps we wouldn't have felt so free to ask. Of course, they knew they had his pensions coming, that their retirement would be essentially salaried—they didn't really need a nest egg—but this radical generosity to us was, nonetheless, extraordinary, and the more extraordinary to me for having been kept secret.

The day Dad left to drive back to New Jersey was frigid, the old snow on the street frozen and grimy. His car, a battered dark-green Volvo parked in front of my house, was packed full of boxes of papers and books. I'd fixed him a lunch for the road. Maybe, he said, he'd save it for dinner when he got home to New Jersey. I thought then of the new absence he'd have to confront there, the empty house, the silence, Mother's things, her arrangements, everywhere.

I went out on the front porch to wave goodbye to him. He was wearing a ratty balaclava and the slightly-too-big tweed coat that my mother had bought for him secondhand somewhere; she had always bought all his clothes for him. He led his old dog out to the car and helped him into the passenger seat—Kolya was by then maybe sixteen or seventeen, an arthritic black Lab mix who'd gone grizzly white from the bottom up. Then Dad crunched around to the driver's side, breath blurring, got in himself, and started the car. I watched them as they rounded the curve out of sight. He honked once. I was tearful again, suddenly stricken with sorrow for all I couldn't do for him, for his solitude, for all the lonely tasks ahead of him. I remember thinking, Please don't, don't let Kolya die for a few more years.

Through the next days and weeks, I tried to reassure myself with the beginnings I had seen. I thought of my father, making his notes, working out the rules for his new life. I thought of a poem I found, complete, in my mother's papers after she died, about the differences between them.

*His habit is to work.*
*Diurnal, steady as the sun*
*He rises, dominates the day, it seems.*
*Lies down at night*
*Stinted.*

*Her habit is to moon about.*
*Waxing, waning—*
*Flux.*
*Some days full-face, smiling, whole.*
*Others attenuated as a nail paring.*
*Written off.*

Surely this is how he would proceed—steady as the sun, *working*—even in his grief.

*     *     *

This was not the way it happened, though. That steadiness, that dailiness, that seemingly permanent temperamental need to be always *at* something fell away from him. And my education into the disjuncture of his dying, its inconsistency with his life, began here too. No wonder I resisted understanding it.

It helped me in my resistance that he seemed much the same *interpersonally* for several years. He was interested in all our doings and stimulated by company, by intellectual events. He and I spoke and wrote often. I kept most of his letters, his script precise and vertical as always. He described things he'd seen and done.

*Reds* [the movie] is well worth seeing. The hero looks like Ben. It's long and sprawling, but finally focuses in on a taut and convincing triangle—O'Neill, Reed, and Louise. And the climax in Russia in the revolution is wild adventure. There is a fascinating chorus of elderly survivors: Eastman, Henry Miller, etc., who reminisce periodically, and Emma Goldman, Lenin, Zinoviev play their parts in the action.

He sent me advice about my new life teaching, about my work:

Don't be intimidated by your students. After all, the incoming freshmen are fresh out of high school and the senior prom. They are enormously different from first-year graduate students, even those who are only twenty-two.

And:

I'm sorry that you were bumped from the advanced writing class. I suppose the dean figures that since he has to pay the full professor's salary anyway he might as well get a full work load out of him. But if you are producing, that's better yet.

He sent me clippings from the paper of things he thought I'd be interested in as well as things that amused him. One about a man who'd 'accidentally' shot his mother-in-law (not badly), claiming he'd mistaken her for a raccoon. Another:

A Hopewell [NJ] man allegedly snipped off the long braided ponytail of a Cranbury woman as she jogged along Pretty Brook Road Sept. 19, about 5:50 p.m. The braid extended down to her waist, according to police.

The woman told police she screamed and the man ran north on Pretty Brook Road. She ran to the nearby Pretty Brook Tennis Club where two staff members and a club member pursued a suspect.

He was cornered by the three hiding in a pond on Princeton Day School property, within a patch of lily pads. The man was held at bay until the arrival of police . . . He allegedly used a pair of scissors in the assault.

I can still laugh out loud when I read this old clipping, so like the germ of a Cheever short story. And it reassured me that my father would notice and be amused by such a thing. He still had his sense of humor then. He still took pleasure in what was offbeat in life, what was Thurberesque.

It's just that he had also pretty much stopped *doing* things. The first summer after my mother's death he never got around to getting a fishing license. He gladly hiked with me and Ben when we visited him in New Hampshire, and with my brothers when they went up; but not on his own, not with that self-propelled interest in the activity that had always marked him. And over the next few years I noticed that things began to come up that interfered with projects and plans he'd made. He'd forget to reserve a kennel spot for the dog and have to cancel a retreat or miss a reunion. He'd just *never quite get around* to arranging to meet my aunt to watch the hawks migrate.

He began, for the first time in his life, to get negative student evaluations. The enrollment in his classes dropped.

> My two courses seem just barely enough, five or six each, so that I can't cancel either. There is one advantage to the light load, in that I am finding it hard to get back into the rhythm of teaching, and to organize effectively.

Within two or three years of Mother's death, he seemed to me to be reduced, slightly withdrawn, increasingly without initiative.

And now the old friends and relatives began to talk to me, that series of conversations conducted, really, behind his back, the questions I couldn't answer: What's *wrong* with your father? Is he lonely? Depressed? What did you notice? Aren't you worried? What are you *doing* about it?

But I talked with him face-to-face too, and at first he was characteristically candid—and insightful and intelligent—about what he saw as his failings. He fooled me, maybe he fooled himself too, by being so open and clear about it. He said he couldn't stay focused in class. He'd begin a thought, and by the time he'd made his way through two or three sentences he would have forgotten where he was heading, and he'd have to do some tricky intellectual footwork to make it seem he'd had a point at all. He said he was making no progress on his writing projects. He laughed at himself, ruefully, for his lack of discipline, for watching too much TV. 'The old man's comforter,' he called it.

It was at the end of this period—six years in all—that my sister and I persuaded him to move to Denver.

*　　　*　　　*

I still don't know exactly what we were seeing in Dad at that time. But whatever it was, I know I pushed it away—thinking about it, trying to understand it, even, sometimes, seeing it. I chose, I think, not to notice as long as I could.

Why? Because, I suppose, he was still so smart, so interesting and interested. Because the disease's onset was lurching, halting, and the good times made me dismissive of the bad times. Because I could argue to myself it was partially depression over my mother's death.

Sometimes I thought that what I was seeing plain for the first time was the lifelong forgetfulness, abstractedness, that had driven Mother slightly crazy but that her compulsive perfectionistic control over their life together had shielded him from revealing. Now of course it was exposed, now that he had to *manage* his life as well as live it. Even I, who had so idealized him, got irritated with him occasionally early in this period for forgetting to do things he'd said he would do—for me, for Ben.

But I also think that at the heart of my not-seeing was my astonishingly naive set of assumptions about death. This could not be what was happening to Dad. Not to *my* father. That he would he diminished, and diminished again, before he died? That I would lose him, over and over, before the final loss? That I was already losing him? Some childish part of me simply said no—this couldn't he the way he would die, he would end—and continued to say no even after it ought to have been clear that it was, indeed, the death he was moving toward.

Now that they're both long gone, it is my mother, the one who died earlier, the one whose death I did not see, whom I sometimes dream alive and whole again. What I imagine in my sleeping life is that it was all a mistake, the notion of her dying—some sort of confusion on our part. And when I wake after these dreams, occasionally I believe in them for a few moments: I believe she is alive.

I never have such dreams about my father, though he comes to me often enough. But the dreams aren't a denial of what occurred in life.

130

Too often, they confirm it. Something terrible is happening to my father in the dream, my father is trying something and failing, my father is speaking and making no sense. And always, always in these dreams, I am useless. In spite of my tortuous, dreamlike efforts, 1 am utterly unable to help him.

## CHAPTER SEVEN

There was another reason to deny what I saw coming—saw, but turned from seeing as long as I could. In the years between my mother's death and my father's diagnosis, my father and I took up our relationship again. We began, I would say, to know each other. Basically it was a matter of learning to talk to each other as we once had, before my mother's anxiety about that made it difficult. A matter of being together enough to grow comfortable with her absence, which initially loomed as large between us as her presence once had.

For both of us, I think, there was some terror about this. Late in the spring after my mother dicd, hc and I took a long trip together, driving across the country in his car with a trailer hooked onto the back, a trailer we had packed with all the furniture and china and possessions, mostly Victoriana, that had come from Mother's family, which my father now thought proper to distribute among her children. The plan was to take about ten days to wend our way from one of my sibling's homes to the next. Anticipating this, I remember thinking, and saying aloud to friends too, 'God, what are we going to *talk* about all that time?' When later in the summer his friend Peggy Grant told me he'd expressed the same fear to her, I laughed at how like each other in many ways we were.

The trip did have its awkward moments, and somewhere perhaps in Pennsylvania I launched myself into a new bad habit as a result of my anxiety, tearing and biting at my cuticles until they bled, a habit I've yet to cure myself of completely. But it was a test of sorts, and we passed it. I remember one particularly David Lynch-like moment on Mother's Day—which we'd both forgotten completely, never having celebrated it in our family (my mother thought it was a bogus holiday). We arrived in a packed roadside restaurant somewhere in Nebraska to discover the Mother's Day brunch coming to its caloric conclusion. I told the dubious man in charge of welcoming us that I was a mother myself and was given a wilted corsage to pin on. He explained that things were winding down and seated us somewhat reluctantly. The waitress came over, seeming irritated, and told us what we couldn't have. And before we had finished eating, everyone else having risen and left nearly as one slightly

132

earlier, a midget began vacuuming the room, slowly closing in on us. We actually had to lift our feet as he poked the roaring machine under our table, never meeting our eyes. Which was just as well, as we were sniggering and choking on our laughter at the absurdity of the whole event.

During the long days on the road we learned to talk in the desultory but intimate way that such a trip makes possible. We spoke of Mother and about Dad's plans for teaching. I talked about myself—I'd had my first stories accepted for publication that spring and was full of the sense of my possibilities. We spoke of my siblings and about the summer coming up. I can't say I wasn't relieved when the trip was over—it was work, it was a strain too—but it changed something between us, mended some rift or gap formed long ago.

I saw much more of my father in the following few years than I had before. We took other long trips together: to family events and reunions, to weddings. We drove to Pennsylvania for a family funeral and stayed on a few extra days with a favorite aunt because my car broke down. We drove to Chicago for a Christmas with two of my siblings and their families and came back together, making our way cautiously through an ice storm that scared both of us. I spent much of each summer with him in New Hampshire. For some of these years I was still

133

single, and I confess I thought sometimes of those nineteenth-century spinster daughters who take care of their widowed fathers into their old age. I knew this wasn't possible for me—I was too committed to my freedom, to my work, to my privacy—but I enjoyed the fantasy. No wonder I denied the first symptoms I saw. The second, the third. Just as I was coming to feel I knew my father again, he began to disappear into his illness.

\*         \*         \*

Our rescue together of the cat house contained both these elements: knowing him and losing him. Here's the story. For many years, since the mid-fifties, my parents had rented one cottage or another in a little town in the White Mountains of New Hampshire where many academics summered. They'd come there originally, actually, to visit friends who lived on our street in Chicago; the husband was a colleague of Dad's at the Divinity School.

A few years after my mother's death, the cottage my parents had spent at least a decade's worth of summers in was offered for sale. Suddenly my father was faced with a decision. He'd wanted for a long time to buy a house in New Hampshire, a place where the family could gather, a place he could leave to all of us, but he'd been perfectly comfortable too in the rental cottage. Now that it was for sale, he had to think about all his options.

The more he thought about it, the more he felt the Stevens cottage didn't make sense. It needed work of a structural sort, and none of us knew how to do it. It wasn't winterized, and he thought a place that could be used year round would be a better investment. He looked at several other cottages for sale, and then he began to focus on the Mitchell cottage. I don't know how he first learned it might be available. It wasn't on the market. It might have been the real estate broker who planted the seed—that this beautiful, derelict shingle house, owned by the deeply eccentric Bill Mitchell, who lived there reclusively with many cats, might be had for a song.

Bill was probably in his late sixties then, though he looked much older. Life had been hard on him. He came from some money, he'd gone to Harvard and then Harvard Law School, but he'd never been able to launch himself into the world, and he was clearly incompetent to manage the vagaries and difficulties of modern life. When his mother died, she left her money in a trust. Bill and his brother were to get an annual allowance. After some years, though, Bill had somehow broken into the trust and began to use up the principal to support what amounted to his addiction: cats. Now he had no more money, and the house was in terrible shape—partially because

135

of the cats, partially because he'd done nothing to maintain it. He was willing to sell it for very little in order to continue to support the cats, all of whom he was going to move into two trailers perched on the land of another animal-loving friend.

When I told a local friend of Dad's interest in Bill's house, he said, 'I wouldn't touch it with a ten-foot pole, and neither should your father.'

But Bill was willing to let the house go for $30,000, and my father had accumulated that much in the years after Mother's death, since he had no expenses to speak of: he didn't buy clothes, he didn't travel, he still drove his old car, he ate simply, his mortgage was paid off. Buying Bill's house outright would mean he needn't undertake a new mortgage—something that scared him. That fear and his vagueness about money management—which might have been reflective simply of his lack of experience or might have been the Alzheimer's—made the Mitchell deal seem attractive.

A complication was that Bill wouldn't let us in to look at the house. He said he wanted to get it cleaned up first; he was ashamed for anyone to see how dirty it was. My gentle father could understand this; he was sympathetic with Bill about it. Besides, we already knew the house was large and beautiful—we'd been in it years earlier, before

Bill bought it. It had six bedrooms and a vast living room, wainscoted to eye level, with a huge stone fireplace at one end. The land below it sloped down to Moose Brook. The wide porch that wrapped its front looked east across the valley and directly up at Mount Madison and Mount Adams. In the evenings the setting sun lighted their rocky peaks orange, then pink, then purple. How bad could it he? We'd have to clean it, we figured—scrub everything, air it out, set off bombs for insects. It would surely smell of cat for a while, but my younger brother, a vet, knew various products that would help with that, as would applying polyurethane to everything in sight. We were all for it, except for my dubious older brother, who was allergic to cats. The rest of us, though, offered to help; we saw it as an adventure. Dad made his offer and was accepted.

But Bill kept postponing the closing. He wasn't well, and he just didn't seem to be able to pull himself together to do the cleanup, which would be step one in putting everything into motion. Step two, obviously, would be moving the cats out, no small project. By his own count, there were more than eighty of them.

Several deadlines came and went. Finally my father gave Bill a kind of ultimatum, combined with an offer to help with moving the cats and cleaning up. Bill reluctantly

137

acceded and they set a date. I cleared my schedule for a few days and went up to New Hampshire.

I arrived in time for dinner at the Stevens cottage.

Well? I asked. How was it?

My father was clearly stunned by the scale of the mess. He couldn't bring himself to describe it; he just said it was 'unbelievable.' He was quieter even than usual at dinner and through the evening, as I chattered on about clean-up strategies and transport for the cats.

The next day my father went down to Bill's house after breakfast while I drove to town to buy equipment: mops, buckets, scrub brushes, cleansers, trash bags. Then, wearing my overalls, I drove to Bill's house too, ready to go. At this point I'd ripped out walls in my own little house in Cambridge, sanded and finished floors by myself, replastered, painted, done primitive plumbing. I knew it all, I thought, and I loved a project.

Nothing could have prepared me for the scene in Bill's house. It was like walking into a deeply perverse ecosystem, an embrowned hell, with the terrified cats, dozens and dozens of them, inbred and bizarre-looking, unused to any other human but Bill, shifting in massive *waves* of feline life with every motion you made. *Shit* was the operative word here, the word no one had mentioned—not even the real estate agent, whom I began to regard from that moment on as fundamentally criminal. (Instead of a percentage, he'd taken as his payment a twenties-era LaSalle Bill had upon blocks in the garage.)

At some point, Bill had given up. Instead of cleaning the shit up, he'd chosen to walk around it and then, inevitably, to step on it. The floor was made of it, ten to twelve inches deep in some parts, we later discovered—and this had come to be the essence of life for a whole happy ecological universe. The cats made the shit; blissful flies bred in it, flew around, and tapped the walls and windows, which were lightly coated in a brown like the darkened glaze of ancient paintings. Spiders nearly as fat as my fist dangled in corners and from the ceiling, barely needing to exert themselves to feast on the flies. The cats had clawed the damask curtains to shreds, here and there pulling them down. The beautiful old furniture was deeply grooved, scratched, gummy with shit. The posts on the elegant open balcony and stairs at the end of the living room opposite the fireplace were clawed to stalactites and stalagmites, only occasionally still meeting in their narrowed middles.

My father's eyes in his defeated face were steady on my own face, which I'm sure revealed everything I felt. It was hideous. It was ruinously awful.

He owned it.

I had a sense at the moment of the transfer

of responsibility, of picking up a burden. He looked whipped. I couldn't afford that, for his sake. Someone needed to say it could be done. Someone needed to *feel* that. All right. All right. It would be me. It was nearly a physical sensation, taking it on. I don't remember, actually, what I said. I know I was furious, but somehow I didn't aim that at my father. Bill, I suppose, felt the brunt of it, but even there I was restrained. I set aside my useless cleaning tools. We decided for the moment to focus on the cats—catching them, putting them into boxes, laundry hampers, crates, anything they couldn't escape from that would also let them breathe.

My father and Bill made the first trips, while I stayed behind, boxing up more of them. At the end of the second day, I made two trips myself up to Stark, where Bill's trailers were set on a hillside, one for himself and the nursing mothers and kittens, one for all the other cats. In the car as I drove, the terrified cats yowled and threw themselves around in their containers. I could see the boxes lurching and bouncing in the rearview mirror, and I prayed, I prayed no cat would escape while I was still on the road.

At one point in the second day, while we were loading them up, Bill got upset. We couldn't go on, he said. This was too hard on them. We just couldn't—

'We're doing it,' I said. No arguing now.

They were going.

At another point in those days, he tried to give me a gift—a box of assorted jellies and jams—to express his shame and his gratitude, he said.

I was merciless. Not for a moment should he think I was doing any of this for him, that anything I was doing was remotely connected to him. I couldn't begin to express my feelings about him, and I wouldn't. And there was no one else on earth I would do this for but my father.

*This*, once we got the cats moved and Bill was gone, consisted mostly of gathering whatever familiar, reassuringly human garbage we could and throwing it away. We emptied the refrigerator and the kitchen shelves, where food was rotted and molding. We cleaned up the empty cat food cans and lids everywhere. We picked up syringes—Bill had done his own veterinary medicine. Meanwhile we pondered and discussed strategies: how to do the rest of it.

Once the original shock was over, my father and I could actually find humor in the situation when we spoke of it. It was so extreme; it was so beyond anyone's imagining. We compared our dream lives, since Bill's house in one form or another had come to dominate our sleeping hours.

The basic task, as we saw it, would be like that of shoveling out a stable—a particularly disgusting stable. In the end we decided teenagers would be our best answer. I thought Ben and some friends might be just money-mad enough, just oblivious enough to take this on.

But it was obviously too late, this year, to do much. School had started. My father had to get back to New Jersey and I to my life of adjunct teaching wherever I could get work in Boston. We decided to let the house sit, unheated, through the winter. At the very least, it should kill off some of the insect life. In the meantime we would organize and gird ourselves for next summer, when we would Get It Done.

I did go up to New Hampshire once by myself on a beautiful day late in the fall. I think I literally couldn't believe it was as bad as I remembered it; or, rather, that my disbelief had been powerful enough to actually alter my memory of it. What I imagined, driving up, was that I'd clean the kitchen or one or two of the bedrooms where only a limited number of cats had been allowed. (One room, for instance, was for sick cats, another for 'bad' cats, Bill had told us—by which I assume he meant murderous.)

When I opened the door, though, I felt the shock of appalled discovery all over again. It was unspeakable. And this time around, the flea population, deprived of its source of food, the cats, found me almost instantly. I felt them on my exposed flesh—their light touch, their bite. I ran outside, swatting and flailing. And then I was aware of them moving on my legs, under my overalls. In a panic I unlaced my shoes and kicked them off, then pulled my overalls down. A roiling black anklet was moving up each leg. Careless of cars going by in the road, I danced around in the overgrown grass in my underpants for a while, raking at my flesh, slapping myself. Finally I got dressed again, locked up the house, got in the car, and started the three-hour trip back down to Boston.

The next June, in the weeks before Ben went off to camp, I ran a kind of alternative camp for him and three friends—Jessica and Kate, whom he'd known since day-care days, and Nikko, an older friend of Kate's who'd just graduated from high school and who was our salvation. He understood the notion of physical labor in a way the other three didn't, they were so young. Weekdays they worked all day each day, though the three younger teenagers could sometimes be heard in the far reaches of the house shrieking and chasing each other around. The syringes in particular they found ghoulishly delightful, but we also discovered trunks full of jewelry and clothing from the thirties and forties that they made piles of to salvage. We used hoes, ice chippers, and shovels to pry up the dried, hardened shit. The cats had knocked many books off the shelves into the mess, and these had been covered over the years: the kids elaborated a fantasy about these new building materials: books and shit, like bricks and mortar, only stinkier.

My father had arranged to pay several hundred dollars a trip for the town garbage truck, and when we had enough barrels full of junk, when we'd piled the dried, hardened shit headhigh in the living room once again, we'd call the collector to come and then run back and forth with the barrels, filling the truck with a combination of ruined furniture and fabrics and trash and barrel after barrel of shit and shit and more shit.

I cooked two enormous meals a day and packed lunches for all of them. In the afternoons when we were done working, we swam in the lake near Bill's house. We bathed again once we got up to the Stevens cottage. The kids washed their clothes out each night so they could stand to put them on again the next day.

Each weekend I drove them all back to Cambridge, usually with a trunk full of booty: old fur coats, white flannel pants, wide ties and dresses from the forties, and the few books, leather-bound and lovely, that hadn't been ruined. But we all ended up throwing a good deal of this away. Even after weeks of airing out, if it couldn't be washed, it still stank.

It was, actually, a lot of fun. In the evenings

144

we played board games or read, sometimes aloud—Sherlock Holmes, for instance. The kids were spirited and energetic. I think they had a sense of adventure about the whole crazy episode. In addition, they could see the results of their labor quickly and gratifyingly. By the third week we were able to start washing walls and windows.

After they were done and had scattered to their various summer activities, I continued to come up each weekend, usually for three days, to work beside my father, scrubbing, patching the plaster, painting. Dad found someone willing to sand the floors—a miracle, given what was embedded in them—and he and I began the slow process of polyurethaning every floorboard in the house. I felt a real ease and companionship working alongside him. In the evenings, at the pristine-seeming Stevens cottage, we read or talked, and it was in these conversations that he expressed to me some of the regrets about how he'd lived his life. He also talked openly and freely, it seemed to me, about Mother, about her depressions and eccentricities, sometimes with regret, sometimes with amusement and delight. We discovered Garrison Keillor on the radio one night that summer, and routinely listened to him on Saturdays as we fixed our dinner and ate it. My father enjoyed especially his commentary on religion and on the Boy Scouts. He often laughed out loud as we

145

moved around the kitchen.

He went to church on Sundays. I usually didn't, preferring to keep working. But we often went to the Sunday-night hymn sings together and sat sharing a hymnal. By midsummer it was clear the house was salvageable; by late summer I was grateful for what working on it together had given to us, to me in particular.

Of course, even that summer there were signs I noticed, symptoms I wondered about. Often I spent the hours he was in church redoing something he'd said he'd finished. Once, for instance, he undertook to wash the upstairs bedroom doors. He was done in record time, but I saw, when I looked at them, that he'd actually only washed a few and even those not thoroughly—and thoroughly was what was required, in the circumstances. I scrubbed them all myself a second time.

And there was the issue of money and its connection to the work—which, after all, was hard and sometimes seemed endless. At one point that summer, a close friend in Randolph asked me why we didn't hire someone to do more of it. 'Surely your father has enough money for that.' But, of course, I didn't know whether he did or not. I had no idea, actually, about his finances at this point. I'd seen them several years before, just after Mother died, but I thought buying Bill's house might have taken him down to near zero again. In addition, I was keenly aware that I'd paid back only a small part of the money my parents had loaned me to buy my house—money, as I now knew, that represented all they had at the time. In a sense, I felt I owed my father my labor, especially if he couldn't afford anyone else.

But there was a moment late in that summer when he took a call from one of my siblings who needed money to buy a house, just as I had once. I was on my hands and knees, scrubbing, when he answered the phone, but I could hear every word of Dad's end of the conversation. It was completely audible to me when he readily agreed to a $12,000 loan.

I was stunned. If there was $12,000 to spare, my father's friend was right—there was a kind of insanity to this tedious, never-ending work on our part. I remember, through that day and in the week following in Cambridge, thinking how strange it was, in a way, that my father could even have *allowed* me to do what I was doing if he had enough money to pay someone else to do it.

I certainly hadn't wanted him to consider my labors a sacrifice—I'd worked willingly, lovingly—but the knowledge that he could easily have hired someone seemed to reveal a kind of callousness on his part about what those labors might have cost me—might be costing me. As I pondered it, I wondered if he was simply so used to my mother's compulsive but absolute self-sacrifice on his behalf that he took my help for granted. Or was it a mark of some new failing on his part, a failing to see, to take in, the effort, the time it was all taking? He knew I was beginning now on my novel, he knew I had a grant, a precious one-year-only grant, that had let me escape from the round of teaching gigs all over Boston to write.

On the other hand, I told myself, what did it matter, really? I enjoyed the work, in fact. There was a part of me that saw this combination of elements in my life—four days focused writing in Cambridge, three days of hard labor in New Hampshire—as more or less ideal. And I was writing well, prodigiously well, when I wrote. If it cost me a little time, well, wasn't that fair, considering his generosity to me in the past?

Still, that blankness about it, that lack of delicacy—the need to work on the house exposed this and made me aware of what seemed to me a lapse in him. Just as, in the next few years, the continuing work there exposed him more and more in his weaknesses, in his increasing inability to follow through with tasks, to think clearly about what needed to be done next and next and next, in his passivity about making decisions.

Even so, even so, I'd do it all again. The house came around, finally. It was livable; then, in another year, enjoyable. And

148

diminished as he was by that time, my father did enjoy it. As I enjoyed his enjoyment. I liked watching him sit in the sunny corner of the living room by the window seat in the late afternoon, listening to Mozart, looking at the birds flying in and out of the blue spruces and the lilac hedge. I liked sitting with him on the front porch in the morning sun with a cup of coffee, talking or listening to the river rush by below us.

And even after he was diagnosed, even after we all finally knew what his failings had been about, the house was a kind of refuge for him. While he was living in Denver, he came east each summer, and I usually spent a month or so up there with him, and each of my brothers were there a week or more. My times were, as usual, quiet. We took walks, we read, we went to church. I continued to work on the house too, but he'd pretty much stopped being able to. We talked. His concerns by now were more tightly circumscribed, focusing on my sister and her children, on the house itself, on me and my life—and he was a bit perseverative about them all: we covered the same ground many times over.

The last of these summers before he came east to live permanently at Sutton Hill, he brought a box of personal papers to New Hampshire with him. Sitting in his bedroom facing the mountains, he spent some time each day going through them one by one, then tearing them carefully into pieces and throwing them away. I recognized the handwriting as I carried his wastebasket down to the trash: they were my mother's letters to him and his to her.

I used this behavior later in a novel. I had a middle-aged man's dying mother destroying her correspondence with her husband. I had the son emptying the trash regularly, as I did, and looking at the fragments of his parents' past—his own history, in a sense—as he bagged them up and threw them away.

My character's situation was different from mine, though. His parents had divorced years earlier, and he yearned to know his now-dead father. He was, in a way, angry that these letters were being taken from him, that he had to collaborate in disposing of them. He felt an intense desire to read what passed through his hands.

I felt some curiosity, of course. I felt too that I held a history, a story, as I lifted the basket and upended it into the mouth of the plastic bag each time. I won't say I was without regret as I hauled the trash out for collection each week.

But I knew my parents—knew enough of them, anyway—so that what I was most aware of was a kind of awe for my father as he carried out this task. Every time I passed his open door (it reminded me of that open study door of my childhood, actually) and saw him there, reading and then carefully tearing the letters in two, then in four, what I felt was a deep and compassionate admiration and also a kind of amazement at his consistency in this one task. That he, who had so much trouble completing almost any other chore, should be so thorough and undeviating in his daily work at this prolonged and permanent farewell to his own life, his past, his love, moved me more than I can say.

## CHAPTER EIGHT

From the time my father arrived back east permanently to live near me in a continuing care retirement community in suburban Boston, he was hallucinatory. This had been only an occasional problem in Denver, so it seems clear that it was in part the difficult transition that triggered it—the transition to a new, comparatively tiny space (he'd had a two-bedroom apartment in Denver with a view to the mountains; here he had one room with a lavatory), to the loss of his books (there was space in his room for only one standing bookcase full, down from a dozen or so in Denver), to the sudden absence of my sister and her children, who'd been part of his everyday life there.

In retrospect, were I to choose a place for

him again, knowing what I know now, I'd choose proximity over programs, over elegance, even over reputation. Because what was hard for me at Sutton Hill was to drop in on Dad for a lot of short visits or to have him over for a quick casual meal—and that's what would have been best for both of us. But it took forty minutes just to get to Dad. And it was harder still to have him visit at my house. To drive out and get him, come back, return him at the end of a visit, and drive home meant three hours in the car. Most weeks I saw him only once or twice.

He was, then, really institutionalized, and it was damaging to him. The progression of his disease from this point on was more rapid than it had been before. He changed, and changed again. And in response, often lagging a step or two behind him, I changed also. Slowly, reluctantly, I learned new ways to behave, and I too was transformed, at least with him, as his illness deepened.

My father never really understood where he was at Sutton Hill. He had to be reminded why he was there over and over, and then he'd forget again. When he first arrived, he could still give a kind of lip service to the explanation he'd understood earlier: he had Alzheimer's disease. Often now, though, saying this seemed a kind of mindless habit, something he'd taught himself to repeat without fully comprehending it. If I specifically reminded him that he was at Sutton Hill because they could care for him through the course of the disease, he'd politely concur. But my reminding him of that was usually and increasingly provoked by his having asked when he was going 'home' or how long he was staying 'in this place.'

My original impulses hadn't been to try to support my father's delusional life. I'd been fooled by my first few experiences with his hallucinations, when I'd been able to talk him out of them, to reason him back to reality. I'd persuaded him that they were the result of fatigue, or of pushing himself too far, or—once we knew he had it—of the disease itself. And at this early stage, when I explained this to him, when I corrected him, he'd been able to step away from his visions, and from himself as their creator, and comment on the oddity of it all. I think I felt a kind of pride in this. I misunderstood it, in my vanity, as a gift I had with Dad.

So for a while after his arrival at Sutton Hill I would try to argue him out of his own perceptions. 'No, Dad, look, when you get close you can see that this is just a reflection, not someone out there watching you.' 'No, Dad, that's just a dog barking, way off in the distance, hear it? It's just a dog, not a person calling.'

Slowly, though, he became unable to accept my version of things. Slowly it became clear to

153

me that my gift was gone. And simultaneously I understood that this was because it had never been mine in the first place, but his—the gift of enough remaining undamaged brain to recognize the damaged part for what it was when I pointed it out. He had lost that now. It dawned on me that my insistence that what he saw wasn't 'real,' that what he heard was not what he thought it was, was making an insurmountable barrier between us, so I stopped.

Now when he spoke of animals in the building or visits from my mother, I would commiserate or be pleased for him. And most of the time I managed to feel these things— the appropriate sadness or pleasure to accompany the delusion. I thought of him as *having had* the experiences he reported. I thought of them as being part of his reality, a part I needed to accommodate and accept. And in the end I did, so thoroughly that it began to strike me as odd when others didn't or couldn't. The nursing staff, for instance, was completely unable to make this leap. When Dad spoke delusionally to them in my presence, they were openly dismissive. They reported his 'mistakes' to me with contempt. This bothered me, more than a little. Had they had no training in the way these events seemed to occur to a delusional Alzheimer's patient? I wondered. Could they not flex their imagination a little bit? Their compassion?

Sometimes the hallucinations seemed painful. One of his recurring ideas, for instance, came because he missed his library, all those books he'd left behind in Denver. Within a few months of his arrival at Sutton Hill, he became convinced someone had stolen them from him, that they were locked somewhere in the basement of the building. He often asked me to come with him to find them.

Tentatively I'd say I didn't *think* they were here and offer my understanding that he and my sister had sorted through and gotten rid of most of them. But this cut no ice with him, so we'd walk around the halls of Sutton Hill looking for the passageway he was certain he'd seen, the one that would take us to the chamber where the books were kept—until we would arrive, to my father's deep confusion, at the activities room or the lounge or someone's office or the country store. A dead end, the remembered doorway now a plastered-up wall, as in some Hitchcock film. (He wandered when I wasn't there too, which bothered the staff, but I decided not to tell them that he was just looking for his books. I knew they'd insist to him that there was no basement and there were no books, and then he'd conclude they were 'in on it'—the theft, the plot.) Sometimes he'd worry about family members, or about other residents, about bad things having happened to them.

155

Most often though, the hallucinations I had to accept as part of his reality were pleasant ones. I've mentioned earlier that my mother came to see him, as did his parents. He reported lively visits from friends. And gradually there came to be a focus to his dementia. The patterns and rhythms that had governed my scholarly father's life asserted themselves here too—from *within* this time— to shape his understanding of his new circumstances: Sutton Hill became some kind of university, a university in which my father's role was multifarious and changeable. Increasingly, when I'd ask him what he'd been doing, what was new, he'd answer that he'd been preparing a lecture. Or that he'd *been* to a lecture (and he did, in fact, go to some in this well-organized community—on transcendentalism, on art history—which probably reinforced the nature of his fantasies). Often he had the sense we get in dreams of being terribly late for something, or terribly unprepared, but more and more of the time now there was one specific context for this—a scholarly context. One time he told me he was supposed to lecture on *Hamlet.* He shook his head. Of course, he knew *Hamlet*, but really, to give a lecture . . . He didn't know if he could do it. It was going to be a real chore to prepare.

He always had a lot of reading to do now to get ready for one thing or another—though in reality, of course, he couldn't read at all any longer—and when I visited he always reported how busy he'd been. Sometimes it seemed he was the professor; sometimes more a student, doing papers, going to class. He wondered, once, when he would get a new room assignment, and I thought he must see Sutton Hill as a college, or perhaps even a kind of prep school.

One of the therapists, a woman who looked a lot like my mother, actually, and whom my father liked, spoke to me of her concern for him. He didn't come to their exercise classes or their musical afternoons or their crafts events. When she passed his room, she always saw him alone, just sitting blankly in his chair or dozing.

I defended his behavior. I said he'd never liked crafts, that he'd never cared for swing music or Glenn Miller—that he didn't even know who Glenn Miller was. (I didn't tell her he'd charmed my mother early on by his unworldliness in pronouncing *boogie-woogie* with soft *g*'s—a detail I once used fictionally.) I said he'd always been relatively solitary. I told her I didn't think she needed to worry about him, because his delusional life was unusually full and satisfying.

I told her I thought he was happy. I still think, at that time, that he was. But perhaps I shouldn't have taken such comfort in what seemed the chance kindness of my dad's illness at this stage. Perhaps I should have wished for him that he embrace enthusiastically the activities offered him, the reality of his situation. That he *go* to exercise classes, that he *learn* to weave or dance. Maybe if he had done those things he would have lasted longer, made more friendships of a sort, and stayed more firmly in touch with all of us too.

But I didn't. I welcomed the sense of usefulness and purpose his delusions gave him. I was glad when he reported he'd done things—familiar Dad-like things—that I knew he hadn't done. I lied. I went along with his mistakes. I still don't know if this was right or wrong, but I would do it again. I would choose to have my father feel happy and competent in some parallel universe, rather than have him build something from popsicle sticks or learn line dancing or reminisce publicly—he who almost never spoke of himself or of his past.

I let him go into his delusion and didn't push him at all into his life at Sutton Hill. I was pleased for him that he'd come home to his own self-invented university.

One afternoon, toward the end of one of my visits, my father said, 'You know, one thing I haven't figured out about this place.'

'What's that?' I asked.

He looked puzzled. 'Well, no one ever seems to *graduate* from here.'

I burst into laughter, so he laughed too, purely at my amusement. He had a wonderful

158

laugh. Not the sound of it so much but its innocence, the way it seemed almost to take him by surprise, nearly to embarrass him.

That night, when I told my husband what Dad had said, he laughed too.

Encouraged, I elaborated on it. I made macabre jokes for my husband in a sardonic W. C. Fields voice: 'Well, Dad, it depends on exactly what you mean by . . . *graduation.*' 'Well, in a certain sense they all do, Dad, they *all* do.'

I laughed, and my husband laughed, and I know if my father had been there—my father as he was before he was ill—he would have too. He would have given himself over, with that surprised, almost startled delight, to the joke he'd made of his illness and laughed right along with us.

\*         \*         \*

If Dad's delusional life had continued in this benign way, it would have been easy for me to continue to accede to it. But as the Alzheimer's disease was progressive, so was the nature of the delusions. Gradually there arose other, stickier dilemmas, ones I had no ready response to, instinctive or otherwise.

He was agitated when I arrived one morning. I asked him what was wrong. There'd been a fire, he told me. A bad one. The residents had all fled the building in their

159

pajamas. (Later I would find out there was, indeed, a fire *drill* in the night, required occasionally by law, and, yes, the residents had gone outside and milled around on the lawn in their pajamas until the all-clear was given.)

'How awful,' I said.

'Worse than that,' he said, 'there were little children killed.' He was nearly trembling, he was so upset.

I looked away. What was I to say now? Could I pretend a grief I didn't have? Could I *act* as upset as he was? 'Are you sure, Dad?' I finally asked.

'Of course I'm sure. I was there.'

I began to back away from this one. 'You know, I don't *smell* smoke. If there'd been a fire, surely there'd be some sign of it, surely we could—'

He shook his head, cutting me off. 'Little children,' he said. 'Dead.' He watched me steadily, waiting for me to recoil, for my eyes to fill with tears, for me to share his pain.

I couldn't. I wouldn't. I felt it would be wrong.

Yet I'd acted as though I believed countless others of his delusions, his hallucinations, hadn't I? What line was I drawing here?

He waited.

I felt accused. 'You know, Dad,' I said, 'maybe it was a kind of nightmare you had. Sometimes they can seem so real—'

'It was no nightmare.' His lips pressed

together. 'There were children who died. And everyone around here acts as if they were just . . . puppies or something.'

I tried deflecting the central point. 'Well, I'm sure the staff is upset too, Dad. But they have to go on running this place. Maybe they can't allow themselves to feel it as much as you do. Maybe they're saving their mourning for later.'

'They are not,' he said sharply. And he looked at me with a gaze as cold and critical as he'd ever directed at me. Clearly he believed I was as inhumane, as inhuman, as they. And worse, that I was an apologist for them, for their attitude.

I found the judgment painful, but I couldn't defend myself. I tried again to express a kind of limited grief, hoping it would temper his disgust. 'I know it must be awful for you, Dad. It *is* awful. And I can't tell you how sorry I am that you had to go through it.'

'I'm not talking about myself,' he said. He seemed indignant at the suggestion. 'I'm talking about little children.'

'I know, Dad, I know. But I was sympathizing with you. With your feelings.'

'That's hardly the point.'

We talked a little longer—or I talked and he stared coldly, at me or just away from me. In the end I left without taking him for a walk, without reading to him or getting his mail or any of the things we usually did.

He was chilly to me the next few times I visited, though I'm not sure he remembered why; we didn't speak of the fire or the children again. But then slowly—mercifully for me—his illness closed over the event or his feelings about it and he forgot my callousness. I didn't, of course, though it was impossible for me to figure out whether there was something I could have done better or differently, some lesson I could have learned from this.

Other times it was clearer to me instantly what I'd done wrong in responding to a hallucination or a delusion, how I should have responded but hadn't. This happened when he fell in love with Marlene.

*     *     *

When Dad went to Sutton Hill, he was at what they called Level Three, a ringer among other residents who truly belonged there. At Level Three you were supposed to be responsible for your own daily hygiene, for your own schedule, for your own laundry and dry cleaning, for your own life. Long before he arrived, Dad was incapable of almost all of this; but Marlene made his Level Three life possible.

I had found her through a list of aides at Sutton Hill, and from the start I held myself lucky. She was in her thirties, a big woman, strong. She had a lovely, softly pretty face, with amazingly white, clear skin. She woke Dad and got him dressed each day; she helped him to shave and to brush his teeth. She did his laundry and took his dry cleaning out. She often took a walk with him. She talked to him easily and sympathetically about her children, about his. She was corrective of his hallucinations and delusions—nothing I said coulcl persuade her to go along with them—but she wasn't insistent or unkind about them. She was protective of him with the nursing staff, too.

Dad often spoke of her affectionately to me, though he never mastered her name with any consistency. Over the year and a half she cared for him, she began to appear in his delusional life. And then slowly she became the focus of it. He would report to me that he'd seen her socially. They went to faculty gatherings together, or lectures, and he was pleased that others in his world liked her, that she was comfortable being among his colleagues with him, in spite of her nonacademic background.

How nice, I would say, when he talked about these events. And then I'd carefully mention her husband or her children. He didn't seem uncomfortable with those references, nor did he seek to deny their existence. It was, I thought, like his simultaneously seeing Mother in his delusional life and knowing that she was dead. In the Alzheimer's brain it seems there doesn't need to be any adjustment or reconciliation between

163

two conflicting perceived realities.

One summer day Dad and I had just sat down in his room to chat. I asked him, as I usually did, what was new.

'Oh, nothing much,' he said. And then, as though just recollecting it: 'Say! I got married!' He laughed, his shy laugh of pleasure.

'Well!' I said. 'Congratulations.' I laughed too, at the absurdity of all of it.

'Thanks,' he said.

'Who did you marry?' I asked.

He didn't look offended. 'Oh, you know.' He couldn't get her name. 'Arlette.'

'Oh, Marlene,' I said.

'Yes.'

'I like Marlene,' I said.

'Yes, she's a fine person,' he said.

'So what else is new?' I asked. And we moved right along. He told me the interesting other twists and turns of the days since I'd last seen him.

I thought no more about it, though of course I should have. It had been, after all, a consistent and prolonged delusional episode— the courtship had lasted several months—with, though I hadn't noticed at the time, a naturally progressive nature. I might have guessed, if I'd thought harder about it, that Dad would take the next logical step after his marriage.

One evening about a week later, I got a call from her. She sounded tense, embarrassed. My father, she said, had suggested that they go to bed together. 'You know, have relations,' she said.

I made some noise in response.

'It didn't really *bother* me, you know. He was very nice about it, really. And I sort of brushed it off. I told him I was there just to be his friend, you know, that it wasn't part of our deal.' But she thought I ought to know, she said, because she'd felt she had to report it to the nursing staff. 'You know, in case it happens with someone else.' She was apologetic. She didn't like to do that, she said. She wanted me to know her loyalty was to Mr. Nichols.

I told her it was I who should apologize to her. That she'd been the center of an elaborate delusion of my father's I should have told *her* about. That I wasn't surprised this had happened because my father had thought he was married to her.

'Oh!' she said.

We talked. I wanted her to know how skillfully I thought she'd handled everything. We ended up laughing about it a little, and after I hung up I was more grateful than ever for Marlene's presence in Dad's life.

The social service worker called the next day to report the event to me. I offered my interpretation, but I sensed she felt I was just making excuses for my father. And indeed there *is* a stage some Alzheimer's patients go through of inappropriate sexual aggressiveness; I had read about it, as I'm sure she had too. I think she felt she was describing this turn in my father's disease to me. But I don't think this is what it was. I think that what happened was born of genuine feeling, not illness. I don't know what the experience of loving Marlene was like for my father—and it's true it was a feeling he might not have had if he hadn't been ill—but I believed then and I still believe that he did love her.

*       *       *

As my father's delusional life thickened and deepened around him, it exacted a price in various ways. One was the loss of his freedom to be alone outside. I'd been pleased when we first looked at Sutton Hill that it was in an almost rural setting, and I think he found it attractive too, when he visited to look at it. There were actually fields, meadows nearly, though they were usually bordered by a stretch of suburban housing. But long walks were possible anyway. And when I first saw the groundfloor room that was to be his, I was also pleased that he had a little patio he could step out onto at any time, an outside sitting space that looked over a garden and then the sloping wooded hills beyond.

For the first months at Sutton Hill he had taken walks by himself, as he'd been used to doing in Denver, and when I came to visit we took them together. By spring, though, by the time he would have made use of the patio, he wasn't allowed out anymore. Twice he'd stayed away too long on his walks, and the staff had to go out to find him. Another time a nurse had found him outside in the garden in the middle of the night—because, as he reported it, he'd heard a dog howling and thought it needed help. The staff felt they couldn't risk his freedom any-more. He could take a walk with me, he could take a walk with Marlene, but the door to his patio was locked with a key, so he couldn't even step outside alone.

Still, we did have pleasant times, pleasant walks—most often to the wildlife refuge at Great Meadows. Compensating for his lack of freedom there were all the activities at Sutton Hill, and I still signed him up for them: we'd go down to the bulletin board and I'd read the choices aloud and he'd indicate what he was interested in. From time to time he was able to take one of these lectures in, really to hear it, and report to me on what it had been about. So at this point, five or six months into his residency, it still seemed worth it to me—the schlep out, the relative inaccessibility, even the strict rules—because of what Sutton Hill offered him.

That next fall, after his return from a stay in New Hampshire with my brother, I signed him up for the symphony, a series of five Friday-afternoon concerts. Sutton Hill had a group that attended together, driven into Boston in

167

the community van. They didn't all sit together—everyone bought a ticket separately, as I had for Dad—and this might be a problem. But the staff agreed to make special arrangements for Dad: one of the residents consented to guide him to his seat and to meet him at intermission; then to wait for him after the performance and walk with him back to the van.

I talked ahead of time to Marlene about the series and asked her to make sure he was wearing a nice shirt and tie each time—no spots, no dribbles. For this first concert, my plan had been to call Dad an hour or two before the van left, to remind him of where he was going that day and to go over exactly what would happen once he got to Symphony Hall. But as I thought about it that morning, I reconsidered. I was never sure how real telephone conversations seemed to him, and I was worried about this event. It was a lot for him to master, in spite of all the planning and help. I decided I'd go out to talk him through the sequence in person.

He did look nice. He always dressed in a jacket and often wore a tie. But on that day Marlene had made sure he looked particularly well put together. He was wearing a herringbone tweed jacket my sister and her husband had chosen for him in Denver, and he had on dress shoes instead of the clunkier, more comfortable ones he usually wore. He seemed to know what was coming. I talked to him a little about the pieces to be performed. I was pretty sure he couldn't understand the notion of musical *movements* in a piece of music anymore, so I advised him to wait to applaud until others had begun—pointlessly, I'm sure; I doubt my cautious father ever led the applause. I suggested, too, that he stay in his seat for the intermission—there would be a lot of confusion then, a lot of people milling around. I told him I'd call him in the evening to see how it had gone.

Through the day I was as anxious as a mother might have been about a child before his first official social engagement. But I was pleased for him, too, and hopeful about this first 'off campus' event he'd attend without me.

At around six, the phone rang. It was the administrator at Sutton Hill calling to tell me that Dad had disappeared at the symphony. He never came to the lobby at intermission, and when the woman in charge of him looked for him in his seat during the second half of the program, he wasn't there. She didn't want to disturb anyone sitting around her, so she waited until after the concert to search for him in the lobby (perhaps he'd felt ill and stayed in the men's room too long?) and then she notified the personnel at Symphony Hall.

They'd scoured the building completely, every dressing room, every closet, and he wasn't there. They'd looked in the immediate environs outside. Sutton Hill was notified and the social worker there called the Boston police immediately. The van had brought the other exhausted residents home. Everyone's best guess was that he was now wandering somewhere in Boston.

After I hung up I called the police too, with a description of my father and what he was wearing. And then I began my vigil, with a series of images playing out into nightmares in my mind before, each time, I willed them to stop.

*     *     *

Perhaps nothing represents more clearly the effect of Alzheimer's disease on the mind than the activity called *wandering*. There's a need to get going, an impulse to travel, but it's disconnected utterly from the notion of destination. It is as though someone had snipped in two the thread that usually connects motivation with activity. Absent also is the sense of pleasurable aimlessness that is part of the *meaning* of wandering for the unafflicted. Purposiveness without purpose, directedness without direction, need without want—these are its hallmarks.

Now I imagined my father striding briskly and anonymously around Boston, a small, tweedy, academic-looking man, completely

170

unremarkable, unnoticeable except for something a little robotic in his gait. How far could he get? How long could he go? Where would he be when he wore down, when he stopped? Who would be nearby, friend or foe?

My husband came home—it was fully dark now—and we talked quickly about who should do what. I thought it made more sense for me to stay by the phone. He volunteered to drive around looking for Dad and, in these pre-cell-phone days, check back with me from time to time.

And so he began his long tours of the various neighborhoods of Boston, tours he would still occasionally recall later with a feeling like that of déjà vu as we drove through some obscure part of town.

There is a sense in which Symphony Hall sits in a central location in Boston, with radically different environments spoking out from it. Back Bay, with its expensive elegant bowfronts and brownstones, shops, and lots of street traffic. Kenmore Square and the Boston University neighborhood, almost as busy, but grungier, petering out into the quiet residential streets of Brookline. The edge of the South End, the varied neighborhood we lived in, sometimes elegant and sedate, sometimes lively with street life, the odd wino or drug dealer. The Northeastern University and New England Conservatory section and, beyond that, Roxbury, Boston's largest black

171

neighborhood.

In each of these areas there were odd forlorn spots, abandoned and sometimes dangerous: the underpass by the Muddy River, the fens along Park Drive, the empty reaches of the Boston Common, the area under the Southeast Expressway near us. These were where I saw Dad in my mind, of course—confused, threatened, mugged, unconscious. And this is the kind of thing my husband imagined too as he drove up and down the streets in each area, slowly cruising, scanning pedestrian traffic, looking for a small man walking, or resting, or hurt, or dead. Every forty-five minutes or so, I'd hear the front door open and he'd call up, 'Anything?' or I'd call down, 'Anything?' and then he'd start out again.

They found him at nine-thirty or so. He'd wandered into Roxbury and sat down to rest on someone's stoop. I don't even know if it was a man or woman who spoke to him, but he or she knew instantly that something was wrong; my father was confused and disoriented. The person called the police and then came to sit with Dad until they arrived.

The police asked for his ID and found in his wallet the card I'd written out for him. *My name is James Nichols. I have Alzheimer's disease. In an emergency call*—and here I'd written Sutton Hill's number and, below it, my own. Since I'd listed it first, it was Sutton Hill

172

they had called. In turn, Sutton Hill called me and told me where he was. We agreed he'd stay the night with me and I'd drive him out the next day.

When I telephoned the police to find out how to get to the Roxbury station house, they said they'd bring Dad to me, and so ten or fifteen minutes later a police car drove up and I ran outside. My father emerged from the backseat. He looked tired, but he seemed pleasantly surprised to see me, and we embraced. I thanked the policemen and asked about the person who'd helped Dad. They had no name, no phone number—just an anonymous good Samaritan. I took Dad inside. The next time my husband opened the door and called up, I said, 'He's here; the police found him,' trying, for Dad's sake, to make this sound unremarkable.

Dad really had no idea that anything was wrong in all this. He accepted that he was spending the night at my house as he'd accepted that he'd been brought to me in a police car—with equal blankness. I asked him about the symphony. It was clear he'd viewed the intermission as the end of the concert. When the music was over, he said expressionlessly, he left.

'But where were you *going*, Dad?' I asked him.

There was a momentary emptiness on his face. And then he said, 'Well, I thought I'd go home, I suppose.'

He was, of course, exhausted and hungry. He said his feet were sore, as if puzzled and amazed that this should be so. After he'd gone to bed, my husband and I sat up for a long time, talking and waiting for the adrenaline that had gotten us through the evening to ebb. And it was perhaps not surprising, but comforting anyway, for us to discover we'd each felt a similar rage when Dad was found, the same kind of rage you feel when a lost child turns up unharmed or a teenager you've imagined dead on the highway arrives cheerfully home three hours after curfew. In the last case in particular, of course, you can vent your anger, you can yell and weep and set draconian punishments. But part of the difficulty with Dad was his childlike obliviousness to our desperation and worry. It reminded me of a time when I was working in day care and a little boy in our group wandered off and was gone for twenty minutes or so at Harvard's Peabody Museum. When we found him, we tried to make him understand how worried we'd been, how much trouble he'd caused, how he could not ever ever do this again. 'You were *lost*, Ian!' we said, trying to make this sound as cataclysmic as possible.

And he pointed out, cheerfully and logically, that of course he wasn't lost; *we* knew just where to find him, didn't we?

The next day, after I'd taken my father back

174

out to Sutton Hill, I telephoned a music-loving friend and offered her the remaining tickets in Dad's Friday afternoon series. From time to time through the fall she'd call me after a concert to thank me again and to tell me about the performers and the different conductors, about the music and her pleasure in it—the very conversations I'd foolishly imagined I might be having with my father.

*     *     *

His progression downhill was slow but steady, but between my efforts and Marlene's we kept him presentable to the community on his floor most of the time. Sutton Hill itself arranged for other residents to call for him at mealtimes, to walk him down to the dining room. Still, he used up more time and caused more difficulties for the staff than the 'normal' elderly around him. His confusion meant that he sometimes resisted routines. He wasn't capable of following instructions of any kind.

His head nurse was a sharp impatient woman who seemed to me to run her wing more for her own pleasure in order than for the patients' benefit. She didn't like Dad. He was messy, a monkey wrench thrown into her smooth-running machine. Several times when I was visiting him, she dropped in uninvited to explain to me what he'd done now that upset the arrangement of things. He was always

175

deferential and apologetic to her on these visits. She ignored him and spoke only to me.

I protested this behavior, finally, to the social service worker. My points: first, that Dad's problems shouldn't be discussed in front of him as though he couldn't hear; second, that my visits with Dad were not the time to discuss him in any case—I'd be willing to come in at any time to talk to the staff separately about him—and third, that the head nurse, as well as the rest of the staff, routinely entered his room without his permission—they knocked once and barged in. I thought he ought to have more privacy.

Everyone agreed with me, about everything. The social worker even ran a special program for the staff as a result of my speaking up, on the possibility of the need for privacy among the residents—privacy to rest or to weep, even, perhaps, to have sex.

But after this the head nurse was chillier to him than ever; Marlene said to me, more than once, 'They're so *mean* to him,' and I wondered then what my stepping forward on his behalf had cost him. I don't know. He never complained. I'm not sure his isolation bothered him. But it can't have helped.

In part, all this resulted from Sutton Hill's not having a separate Alzheimer's unit where Dad's behavior wouldn't have been so potentially offensive or bothersome to other residents. Here it clearly was. He had no

176

friends. I'd heard other residents speak sharply to him more than once, as though his confusion was a result of his not *shaping up* somehow, not trying hard enough. And there were episodes bound to offend others. He wandered upstairs once, entered another resident's room, and lay down on her bed. When she returned and found him there, she was frightened and outraged. She felt he'd done this deliberately, that he'd had some sexual intentions toward her.

The social service worker who called to tell me about this was easy about it, even amused, and I laughed with her on the phone. But after I'd hung up I worried about what the head nurse's take on this would be, how she would talk about it to my father and to the other residents, how the gossip about it would further damage my father's fragile social status.

*     *     *

One day, when I came in, he was agitated. After I'd sat down, he said, with some pressure in his voice, that he needed to tell Sue something.

I said I was Sue.

He looked panicked. 'Well, yes, I know,' he said. 'But I meant the other Sue. I need to get in touch with her.'

'Another Sue? Or Sue Miller?'

'No, Sue Miller. I need to tell her something.'

We went round the confused circle at least once more before I gave up trying to persuade him I was the very person he was thinking of and suggested he dictate to me whatever he needed to tell Sue, and I would see she got the message.

He began, with long pauses between nearly every word. 'Dear Sue,' he said. 'I am writing to the one we know as Sue. To be in touch . . .' I waited. 'So that Sue can hear what I need to tell her . . .'

'Which is?' I asked, after a long moment.

'That I need to be in touch with Sue . . .'

And so it went, only the need being announced, never the message, though we sat for fifteen minutes or so and I carefully wrote down each fumbling word.

It seemed to me, thinking about it afterward, that what had happened was that his memory of me and the person he saw and recognized as me when I visited him had somehow sheared off from each other. And of course it's true that any person you know well has multiple ways of existing in your mind. The Sues in his brain, I thought, were not all one Sue. Oddly, sadly, I also felt he was getting at something else, a deeper reality, in his confusion. For in my treatment of him, I *had* become another Sue—a caretaker Sue. A cheerful, dismissive Sue. A Sue who, from his perspective, was grossly insensitive to the shocking and astonishing and sometimes painful things that went on daily in his universe. A Sue who had taken his car away from him, who was inattentive when he said he needed—had to have—new glasses, when he told her his books were missing—gone, probably stolen!

If he was altered, I thought, so was I—and strangely, in some of the very same ways he was: made bland and callous, *reduced* by Alzheimer's disease.


## CHAPTER NINE

We moved him again, to Level Four at Sutton Hill: nursing care. In the name of helping him, we gave him a new room configuration to learn, a new hallway shape to negotiate, a new staff. All, of course, guaranteed to thicken and deepen his confusion. Perversely, too, no one had told me until the day I went in to supervise the moving of his possessions to the new space that his old familiar chairs, chairs in which he sat and dreamed for hours at a time, would need to be recovered with a fire-retardant fabric for the move to Level Four, and that his desk couldn't come with him at all because it had sharp corners.

Stripped of these personal elements, his

179

new room offered little in the way of charm or comfort. The chairs Sutton Hill provided until I could get his own chairs recovered were from the day room—wood and plastic, small and rather upright. The new hospital-type bed he had now was higher than his old one, with crib sides that flipped up—not a place you could feel comfortable sitting or pass off as a kind of couch, as we had with his bed at Level Three by pushing it up against the wall and covering it with cushions. Of course he had his television—which he could no longer operate; his bookcase—with the books he couldn't read; and his radio—which I always found tuned to soft rock when I came in, in spite of the note I taped to it asking that the staff keep it on a classical music station.

Within days, almost literally before my eyes, the move that was to have helped him in the course of his disease accelerated it dramatically. He became radically more demented. Perhaps the worst element in all this from his perspective was the sudden disappearance of Marlene.

I had known this would come eventually. I understood even at the time I hired her that she was underemployed, doing parttime work with Dad and a few other patients at Sutton Hill. She'd been looking all along for a real job, one with a salary and health benefits. Disastrously, she found it just now. The plan was that she'd leave the week he made the shift. So the one person he counted on daily would not be there. The woman he'd decided he loved would come to see him no longer.

Of course, from a management perspective it worked out well. All the things Marlene had done for him—except for their walks together and her loving-kindness—would now be part of the daily routine care the institution offered at Level Four; even if she'd stayed at Sutton Hill, she would have been a smaller part of his life. But I'd hoped she'd consent to take a walk with him still, to spend perhaps a half an hour a day with him. I was sorry for him that this wouldn't be possible.

I tried to speak to him of the coming changes, as Marlene did. I hired another woman, Nancy, a woman Marlene recommended, to visit with him and to walk with him daily. I hoped, since he hadn't spoken for a while of being married to Marlene, that his delusion's intensity, and maybe even its content, had faded.

Whether or not it had didn't matter. In the midst of everything else about this change that was difficult, unworkable—wrong—was his bitterness and heartbreak over losing her. When I mentioned her name one day shortly after the move, he looked stricken. 'She cut me dead,' he said. His mouth made a bitter line. Even after I'd defended her, even after I'd explained everything to him all over again (she'd found another job, she had to take it,

181

she needed the money, the insurance) he shook his head sadly and said it again: 'She cut me dead.'

I kept thinking there was something I could do that would help him. I went out every day for the first few weeks he was on the new ward—as I couldn't help but think of it. I walked him again and again around it, talking about where things were, then leading him back to his room, next to which I'd affixed a conspicuous sign with his name on it in large print. I repeatedly showed him his bathroom, the lounge, the dining room—a different one now from the elegant space I'd sometimes joined him in for a meal. Here, in the Level Four dining room, many of the patients had to be helped to eat and there was minimal conversation, other than the kinds of words usually used to encourage infants and young children at table. I sat through exercise classes, sewing his buttons on, stitching the required labels into his underwear and socks (the laundry was done for the residents at Level Four), while he half participated at the instructor's enthusiastic commands. I took him for walks outside in the chilly March air.

In some ways, he responded to me as he always had. He was glad to see me. He welcomed the opportunity to chat. But his attention span had, almost overnight, shrunk dramatically. And there were other signs that things were not going well. Occasionally now

182

when I arrived he was in restraints—in effect, tied down to one of the little chairs in his room. When I asked why, the staff spoke euphemistically. *He'd gone a little wild*, they'd say. *He'd gotten upset.* I would untie him, talking to him all the while, and he'd be fine with me.

Sometimes I'd find him pacing the halls, often clinging oddly to the walls, or even crawling briefly, it seemed to get under something. He suddenly *looked* more demented too, in part because on Level Four his laundry was done for him and rough-folded, not ironed, as it was when Marlene had done it; he was rumpled and disheveled-looking. Also, the rule was that patients like Dad, who couldn't dress themselves, had to wear a slipperlike kind of shoe, easy to get on and off. This made him look only partially dressed to me.

He wore diapers all the time now, and even so I would find jackets or ties smeared with shit in the pile of dry cleaning I took away each week. Ties! jackets! I couldn't—didn't want to—imagine how this happened. Nancy reported that he often wanted to ride in a wheelchair on their 'walks.' And then that he'd resisted her once physically, so that she could no longer take him outside except into the inner courtyard—mostly now they walked in the hallways.

And then one day he refused to return to

the building when I was taking a walk with him. It was a damp, gray, mean New England day in March, and he had kept turning away from me on our stroll around the grounds, walking a little distance from me, seeming distracted, as if he heard or saw something I couldn't. At one point he went very close to a little dropoff, a fieldstone container wall, and I panicked. I put my arm through his to try to pull him back from it, speaking to him in what I hoped was a reassuring tone. He didn't respond to me. He was looking out at the horizon line, and his body resisted me utterly. I pulled a little harder, and he froze.

I put my arm around him, turning him physically back toward the building. Slowly I managed to ease him toward it, one painful step at a time, talking, talking steadily the whole way, a nonstop stream—the same reassuring voice I'd used with frightened or angry kids in day care. Cajoling, scolding, entreating. His body was unyielding, and my arms grew strained. My back ached. It seemed to take forever, but I finally got him inside. Things didn't get any easier there, though. Every step down the corridor, he resisted; he pulled away. He was remarkably strong. When his eyes met mine, there was rage in them and no love, no recognition.

We were almost at the entrance to the ward when he turned violently, yanking himself toward the doorway to some offices. I pulled him back, ferociously. In a fury, he charged me, slamming himself against me. My arm bent back and I stepped away momentarily, shocked by the pain. Then I redoubled my grip. We stood looking at each other, locked in our strange embrace. Both of us were panting. He said, 'You don't know who you're dealing with,' in a tone of such hatred, such contempt, that I nearly recoiled.

But I was angry too, simply because he'd hurt me, because he'd fought me. And I was stubbornly determined to get him back on my own.

Why? Partially, anyway, so they wouldn't put him in restraints again or tranquilize him. But I think too that some of it was useless pride: I didn't want to admit to the staff that he'd crossed this line with me too—that he could *not know me*, that he could be as violent with me as he sometimes was with them.

So we slowly did our hurtful dance, inching our way to the ward doors, and then down the hallway in the direction of his room. But at the doorway to the day room, I turned in with him. I felt I simply couldn't make it any farther. My shoulder was throbbing where he'd bent my arm backward, and I knew my back was in trouble. We made our way to a cushioned bench and sat down. I think we were both exhausted; I know I was. We sat silently for a while, side by side. Our breathing slowed, I could hear it.

I watched his rageful, closed profile. Finally I spoke. I told him I knew he was very angry at me, and that I'd been angry at him too. But I felt I'd needed to bring him back where it was safe, and I'd done it because I loved him and cared about him.

He didn't answer me. He wouldn't look at me.

I told him I thought I should go now, that I didn't think we could have a good visit while we were both so upset. He said nothing. I kissed him and left, letting the nurses know on my way out where he was.

\*     \*     \*

Was there a lesson in any of this, anything to take away? What I saw, right or wrong—what I despairingly concluded—was that my presence didn't matter. While perhaps sometimes it was comforting to Dad (though this time, obviously, clearly not), it didn't and couldn't ever change anything. This was a lesson I had to learn over and over with my father's illness, even up to the end: that it would be progressive no matter what I did, that he would get worse no matter what I did. I think this is the hardest lesson about Alzheimer's disease for a caregiver: you can never do enough to make a difference in the course of the disease. Hard because what we feel anyway is that we have never *done* enough. We blame

186

ourselves. We always find ourselves deficient in devotion. *Did you visit once a week? you might have visited twice. Oh, you visited daily? but perhaps he would have done better if you'd kept him at home.* In the end all those judgments, those self-judgments, are pointless. The disease is inexorable, cruel. It scoffs at everything.

Still, still, we look to ourselves to have made a difference. We remember everything we didn't do. This gets played out in painful ways in families too, when one person takes on the caregiving responsibility. Sometimes I wished my siblings would do more—as though that would have made any difference! Just as, when my father was in Denver and my sister had responsibility for him, she felt we others didn't do enough. It is costly, emotionally, to watch someone move inevitably, step by step, into a dementing illness, and it's hard not to want to blame someone—ourselves most of all. But it's useless. At this point in my father's disease, I tried to talk sense to myself. I told myself I had to realize that what I did made almost no difference to him, that aside from the momentary pleasure he took from seeing me at the start of a visit, nothing that happened between us even registered much with him anymore.

I dropped back from the daily visits. By early April I was going usually only twice a week. Then I got the first call. Was I free?

Could I come right away? Dad was in a prolonged violent episode, and they thought maybe I could calm him without a struggle so they could get him tranquilized. And of course I got up, put my coat on, and drove out.

How many times did I go out in all? Five or six, over those weeks, several times from our house in the country where I'd gone to try to get some work done—a house we'd bought in part because it was only a little over an hour and a half away from Dad. My husband came with me one time, and I could feel his appalled shock at the vision of Dad that confronted us: tied down to his chair—which my husband hadn't seen before—slow to register our presence, slow to come around from his angry terror. My husband had thought he would help me, but in the end he let me do it all: hold Dad, talk to him, untie him, sit next to him, rock him when the attendant came in to administer the shot that would release him into calm and then sleep.

Sometimes I was able to calm him myself by reading to him. Certain cadences, most often the Bible (once, oddly, Simone Weil in translation), seemed to work. Sometimes I sang. Sometimes I just held him and stroked him, as you would a frightened child who'd just waked from a nightmare.

The fantasies he had in this period were violent ones. He was being attacked. 'They' were coming to get him, and he needed to arm

188

himself in preparation. He showed me once what he would use: clothes hangers from his closet. 'That's all that's left to me,' he said bitterly.

I didn't know then that aggression and disruptive behavior are often signs of physical discomfort in an Alzheimer's patient. Now that I do, I suspect my father was in pain during these episodes, but that he himself had no understanding of this in a conventional sense and certainly no way to say, 'I hurt.' Instead he incorporated the pain into his delusional life. 'They' were hurting him—badly. 'They' needed to be fought off. And when he fought them off, 'they' needed to restrain him, to tranquilize him, in order to maintain some kind of order for the sake of the other patients on Level Four.

Once—somehow, I think, sensing the truth of the matter—I did think to ask him if he hurt somewhere. He said he did.

'Where?' I said.

He couldn't answer me.

I began to touch him. His shoulders. 'Here? does it hurt here?'

He didn't answer.

He seemed to grunt in the affirmative when I touched his belly, and I reported this to the nursing staff, but when they questioned him he was unresponsive, so we all let it go.

\*     \*     \*

Even on the 'good' days now, when I visited unsummoned, he was more deeply out of touch. Often he'd be in his cruising mode, sometimes carrying something—a book, a bundle of dirty clothing. His walk by now was an odd Parkinsonian shuffle, but *driven*, as though someone were pulling him forward slightly faster than he wanted to go. And of course there was the stopping to strategize about how to get around the things he imagined in his way.

He'd slow down in his lucid moments, sometimes long enough to have the start of a cordial conversation. But he couldn't be held to that for long. Sometimes I'd lure him to his room for a while and talk with him while I could, or read, or sing. But then the other lure, the siren song of his compulsions, his anxieties, would reach him, and he'd want to move again. I'd walk with him as long as he seemed aware of me, as long as it seemed we were, in fact, walking together; but when he lost track of me, I'd tell him goodbye and leave quickly.

This whole period—the period after he moved and when he seemed to retreat so profoundly and rapidly into his illness—lasted only for a few months. I did what I could, starting with the daily visits and at the end going out only a few times a week. After all, as I told myself, I had my own life too. I was trying to work during this period—trying and not succeeding very well. I was starting on a new novel, my third. I'd been starting, I felt, for four or five months. I was very upset about my father, but I was also desperate about my work. I felt miserable, ineffectual in every part of my life.

Late in April I decided I needed to take a break from Dad. I resolved to go if I were called by the nursing staff, but otherwise I'd stay in the country for at least a full week and try to work in a sustained way.

It was nine days before I saw Dad again. I stayed in Westport, alone. I got a lot done. Not once did the phone ring from Sutton Hill. A good sign, I thought. This had been a good idea.

I breezed in again about nine-thirty on a lovely spring morning, waved hello to the nurses, and went straight to Dad's room.

I was shocked. Dad was still in bed, still asleep in the restraints they used to keep him from wandering at night. I leaned over and spoke to him. He seemed to hear me, he turned to me and made a noise, but he didn't truly wake up. He was unshaven. His color was awful. He looked dead.

I went back to the nurses' station, my heart pounding. Why wasn't my father up? What was wrong with him?

Oh, they were sorry, they didn't know I was coming, but he'd had a little bug, a fever, and they thought they'd let him sleep.

191

How long? I asked. How long had he been sick?

Just yesterday and today, they told me.

But why hadn't they called me?

Because they didn't want to bother me, they'd already called me so often.

And what was the bug? What did the doctor say?

Actually, he hadn't seen the doctor yet. She was away, on vacation until tomorrow. They couldn't really tell what was wrong, but it didn't seem bad. He'd been coughing a little, he had a fever. That was all, they thought. A little bug.

I told them it seemed like more than that to me: I couldn't really wake him.

Oh, no, they said. He'd been up yesterday. If I wanted to wait, they'd come down now and get him up and dressed, and I could help him eat a little breakfast.

Yes, I said. I'd wait. I went into the day room and sat down, my thoughts swirling.

I was even more upset when they brought him to me. He was, after a fashion, up and walking—that is, he was vertical; his feet were moving. But it took two of them to support him, and his head was lolling, his eyes partially closed. It seemed to me that he was still not truly conscious.

The head nurse—one I liked in this case—brought a wheelchair for him, and the two aides lowered him into it. I tried to speak to

192

him. It was clear that he could hear me. He turned to my voice again, his eyes opened a little, and he made noises in response. But he never really threw off his unconsciousness. I realized that what he reminded me of was my grandmother, dying. And that's what I thought: that he was dying. I'd thought it the moment I saw him. Something had come to him quickly, some disease, and he was dying.

After he ate a little—he could chew, he could swallow—I pushed him out into the courtyard in his wheelchair and we sat together for a while in the sun. The air was gentle, cool and humid and lovely. I talked to Dad about it, about how wonderful it felt, about spring. A man, a former priest who sometimes visited one patient or another as a volunteer, came up to us, delighted to see Dad, and tried to talk.

Dad didn't respond. 'He's ill,' I explained. 'I'm not sure exactly with what.'

I could see the man was taken aback at how Dad looked and was behaving, and oddly that relieved me—the sense that someone else besides me thought something was gravely wrong here. When I wheeled Dad back inside, I asked that the staff put him to bed, and then I went to talk to the head nurse again. I told her I thought my father was very ill. I told her I was shocked that he hadn't seen a doctor, given that. She was apologetic; he'd been so much better yesterday. And she had already put a call in to the doctor. Dad would see her first thing tomorrow, before she did anything else post-vacation. I stayed for the rest of the day, giving Dad liquids, feeding him again, but he didn't ever truly wake.

Everything seemed a little crazy to me: Dad's nonresponsiveness, the nonresponsiveness of the staff, my own conviction—I understood what it meant just then, to feel something *in your bones*—that he was dying. It wasn't rational, but I knew it. I knew it.

When I went home that night, I called everyone—my siblings, my father's one remaining sister—and told them I thought Dad was dying. By their responses, I could tell they thought I was a little crazy too.

What did the doctor say? my aunt wanted to know. She was herself a nurse.

He hadn't seen the doctor yet, I said.

Ah. Well. Would I call back, then, after he'd seen the doctor?

Yes, I said. I would.

I got out there the next morning before the doctor arrived. Dad seemed the same to me, not unconscious but not conscious either. I sat by his bedside and waited for her arrival.

I had never liked this doctor. I'd chosen her from the roster of doctors available at Sutton Hill because she was a woman. Dad had had a young woman doctor in Denver, the one who had diagnosed him, and he and my sister had both liked her very much. It had seemed to me

194

at the time I made my choice that having another woman physician might help him in his transition to Sutton Hill, might be reassuring to him. But defying all gender stereotypes, this woman was cold and brusque, as unlike my sister's description of his Colorado doctor as she could have been.

When she arrived, she was again cold, almost rude, I felt, even under these circumstances. Her first concern was to establish that no one had called her—that my father's having been allowed to descend this precipitously into illness was not her fault.

I felt a contemptuous rage for her. I understood that, I said. And no one on the staff had blamed her.

She examined him. When she pressed his abdomen, he cried out piteously.

After she'd finished, she turned to me and began to explain my options in a businesslike way. She could hospitalize him for tests. There was the distinct possibility that they'd have to do some exploratory surgery on his abdomen; she thought cancer was likely. And maybe they could repair what was wrong or treat it. But the shift to a new place, the hospitalization itself, the surgery, the drugs, all would be aggravating to the Alzheimer's disease, would certainly intensify his deterioration, and offered no assurance of physical recovery.

The alternative was to do nothing. To keep him here, keep him on antibiotics, keep him comfortable—he would have hospice care, essentially. But because he wasn't really conscious enough to eat, he would die within a few weeks. If this was what I wanted, I would have to sign a DNR—a Do Not Resuscitate order—and the process would begin. She was silent for a moment, and then she said the only even remotely kind or sympathetic thing I ever heard from her lips: 'I know this is hard.'

She meant the decision, but she was wrong. Other things were hard, would be hard, but the decision wasn't. Over the years, Dad had signed several living wills, stating his desire to be allowed to die if he couldn't live with dignity, stating his wish that if he were terminally ill with no hope of recovery, no extraordinary measures should be taken to keep him alive. My sister had told me that at least once he seemed to be asking her, in a roundabout way, whether she would actively *help* him die, something she had felt was out of the question for her—as it would have been for me.

But this, the descent of an illness, an illness whose arrival he'd been too deranged to report to anyone, an illness that through the staff's and my inattentiveness had been allowed to progress to a point where it was threatening his life—this was different. Part of what I'd felt the day before when I'd concluded he was dying was *relief* for Dad. A kind of joy, really. His body was so strong, his heart so good, his health so generally solid, that I had thought he would live until the Alzheimer's disease wrecked him utterly, made him forget how to move, to breathe, to eat. I had thought I would be caring for him in a vegetative state for a long time before the end.

It seemed to me he had already endured a multitude of humiliations and losses, that there was virtually no indignity he hadn't faced—and yet I knew we'd barely begun. That he should die now, that he should die naturally and quickly before he lost completely his sense of who he was, who he'd been, this seemed to me a pure boon, a generous and unexpected gift, the answer to the prayers implicit in the formal, formulaic language of his living will. In fact, I had lain awake much of the night before in a state of nervous tension, hoping this would be possible, hoping my sense that my father had begun his dying was correct.

Hoping, and feeling simultaneously a sense of gaping loss. And shame too: shame for hoping it, and shame connected to my having stayed away too long. If I'd visited a few days earlier, surely I would have sensed the gravity of this illness. Surely I would have had him seen by a doctor—any doctor—sooner, and we wouldn't have arrived at this point yet.

But we had arrived. We had. And guilty as I felt, terrified as I was, shamed as I felt for feeling it, I was *glad*. I was glad that my

197

father's body had found the way out, the reprieve from what had been waiting for him.

I told the doctor that I'd already thought about this and I wanted to sign the order. She said she would have it prepared. I asked her how long it would take him to die. She said she wasn't sure, that it depended a little on how long he continued to eat and drink. Maybe a week, maybe several. She said she'd instruct the nurses that he was to have no pain; he'd get regular morphine. She said she was sorry and then she left. I never saw her again.

I stayed with my father the whole day, feeding him a little, giving him liquids. I left the room when they came in to turn him and change his bedding, but from the hallway I could hear him cry out.

Before I left that evening, I stopped at the nursing station and signed the DNR.

That night, at home, I called everyone again. This time they believed me. I could hear the shock in their voices—some of it, I think, at me, at my choice. I could hear that most of them didn't share the sense I had of a kind of frightened elation for Dad, on his behalf.

*        *        *

So it began. Every day I rose and dressed and had my breakfast, and then, as if I were going to a job, I drove out to Sutton Hill, feeling frightened and weepy each time I drew near.

Once I arrived it was better. I held him, sang hymns to him, or read to him, mostly scripture, a lot of psalms. I brought tapes of the music he'd liked to listen to in New Hampshire and played them. Sometimes I just sat silently by him. I fed him, as long as he could swallow food. I gave him water and juices, at first from a cup and then, when that became impossible for him, from a straw, releasing it drop by drop into his mouth.

The nursing care was wonderful through all this, except for the morphine, which I sometimes had to fight for. But he was always clean, and the women who handled him were tender and loving, sweetly solicitous, especially when they had to cause him pain, which happened whenever they moved him.

My husband came out with me twice. Ben came once. But most of the time I sat alone with him. It took him ten days to die. The organism wants life—clings to it desperately, in fact, whatever the terms—even when the intelligence has decided that the terms are so degrading that death is preferable.

Every morning on the drive out—beautiful day after beautiful day, as I recall them—I was terrified that I'd arrive and find him already dead. It seemed to me part of a pact I'd made, with him and with myself, when I signed the DNR—that I would be with him throughout. That he wouldn't die alone. The thought that he might made me wild. One morning, after

I'd gotten off the highway and was nearing Sutton Hill, a bird flew into my windshield with a loud *thunk!* My heart lurched. As I drove away, I could see it on the road in my rearview mirror, a flopping motion, then stillness. It was a sign, I thought, and began to cry. But when I arrived, Dad was still alive, shrunken now, his nose enormous in his face, his hands held up like claws on the sheet, but breathing. Snoring loudly, in fact. I was so grateful I kissed him over and over.

In all this, I tried to imagine what I would want, dying. To feel loved, I thought. To feel connected to those I had loved. So I held him. I stroked his face, his hands. I kissed him. I spoke the names of the people he'd loved: my mother, his parents, his children, his siblings. The last few days, as his body labored, I told him over and over it was all right to let go, that he didn't have to work so hard. By then, I think, he wasn't conscious. He probably didn't hear me at all. But I kept doing it, in part, I suppose, as a kind of consolation for myself.

He died early in the afternoon on the tenth day, breathing more deeply and slowly, then pausing for a long time between breaths. Then one last breath, and I knew he was gone. His color changed, nearly instantly. He was suddenly, palpably, *absent.*

All the grief I'd held in for days—really, for years—poured out of me. I didn't care how loud I was. At some point, one of the aides came in, then quickly left. The head nurse came a moment later and sat with me awhile, and then the kind woman in charge of social services replaced her. When I finally felt ready to leave, I called my husband, and he came to get me.

At home, I went upstairs to lie down, to weep some more. I had called one of my brothers from Sutton Hill and asked him to call my other siblings. My husband offered to call a few other people—some of my friends; his parents. I could hear his muffled voice rising from downstairs as I lay in our room. At one point, talking to his mother, he laughed about something they'd moved on to, and I felt a shock, a jolt: life went on, then, for others. It would, of course, go on for me too, but at that moment it seemed an impossibility. I felt locked into this grief, as though I'd never get out I couldn't imagine, actually, wanting to. Dad's dying had been like a long labor, the work mostly his, but the experience for me as profound, as isolating, as the labor of birth. For weeks after my son was delivered, I remember, I was stunned by it—by what I'd gone through, by how alone with it I'd felt, by how astonished I was by it, and by how isolating that astonishment was. Others held my son, admired him. They saw him simply as a big healthy baby. But when I looked at him, part of what I saw and felt was how he'd come to me, that long solitary labor, the amazing

201

combination of agony and release that I felt I could explain to no one else. And in some nearly parallel way, this is what I felt about my father's death. It was what I returned to frequently, it was privately *where I lived*, for a long time after it was over.

\*　　　\*　　　\*

For a variety of reasons, my siblings wanted to wait to have a memorial service until the middle of the summer. I argued for something immediate, but my energy was depleted, and I didn't bring much passion to the argument, though I felt passionate enough about it. When I told my older brother that for myself, I wanted, I needed, some ceremony earlier than that—*now*—he suggested I could scatter Dad's ashes. Would that help? *Yes*, I said, though I wasn't sure it was the case. *Yes, I think it would.*

And so my husband and I drove up to New Hampshire with the wooden box I'd requested my father's ashes be put in. (Why had I chosen this? A useless expense in some ways. But I think I remembered the flimsy cardboard box Mother's ashes had come in and felt I wanted something different, something more solid, even though in the end it would have held my father's ashes for only a matter of days.) We stayed overnight in a pleasant hotel and got up early. The ashes were to be scattered according to my father's instructions at a spot

202

high up on the Androscoggin River where my parents had often gone together; my father would fish, my mother would read, the old dog would wade or hunt or sleep on the grass. My mother's ashes had been scattered there, and though I hadn't been present for that ceremony, I knew exactly where it had taken place. I'd gone often enough to the same spot with my parents for picnics.

But when we arrived—on a beautiful clear day, the air still cool and damp—the whole site was crowded, crowded with people with fishing gear. They stood on the rocks, casting off; they waded in at the edge of the rushing water and dropped their lines in the stream below them. It must have been the opening, or near the opening, of the fishing season. Initially it struck me as funny and sad and perhaps entirely appropriate that this should be so.

I moved around carefully among the congregation of fishermen, excusing myself, trying not to get in the way, reaching again and again into the plastic bag that held what was left of my father and scattering it—into the gunmetal rushing water, onto the rocks where he'd stood to fish, then back in the flat clearing where my parents had sat together and had their picnics. The fishermen clearly knew what I was up to. They stepped away from me and called their dogs in as I worked my way around the site.

I tried to be quick, to be minimally

intrusive. I was glad to be doing it, glad to be the one to do it, but its peculiar and public nature robbed it, for me, of some of what might have been healing in it. Or maybe I had exaggerated in my own mind what might have been healing. In any case, when it was done and we drove away, I felt none of the sense of relief, of having ended something fittingly, that I'd hoped for.

In fact, for several years after this I continued to suffer from what I think of almost as seizures of grief, unexpected and uncontrollable bouts of sorrow and rage, triggered by the memory of my father's helplessness in his illness and my own in response. I began to have those dreams of him, the dreams in which he was in some situation he couldn't manage, in which he needed my assistance; the dreams in which, in one way or another, I always failed him. I thought of them as *Alzheimer's dreams.*

None of this was startling to me—that I was haunted by him, that I couldn't let him go. But the way I thought of him and of myself in relation to him began to run on such a well-worn and circular track that I recognized it finally as obsessive. I tried therapy. The talking cure. And it did help with my anger—at my siblings for not coming to see my father while he lay dying and for postponing his memorial service after he'd died; at the doctor who never returned to his bedside once I'd signed the Do Not Resuscitate order; at the sweet and stupid nurse who withheld his morphine because it wasn't 'good' for him; at the Sutton Hill preacher who, in spite of my protests, woke my father to semiconsciousness and pain in order to pray 'with' him; and at myself—for everything I'd done and hadn't done. It relieved a lot of the anger, but it didn't stanch the sorrow, which could still overwhelm me from time to time.

At some point, then, I decided it might help me to make an account of my father's life and, to a larger extent, of his dying. I wanted to scatter his ashes both more publicly and more privately. I wanted to write about him. The purpose of it all, as I imagined it then, would be to help someone else in my position. Someone who found herself taking care of a beloved parent as he disappeared before her eyes, leaving behind a needier and needier husk, a kind of animated shell requiring her attention and care—care she would offer in memory of the person who once lived inside it. I wanted to remember him and also to make some use of his long and terrible dying. I wanted, of course, to heal myself too. And so I started.

# AFTERWORD

Of course, it was not so simple. I started three times during the next decade, and three times I stopped, halted by the sense that I was somehow off on the wrong tack; and then too by an idea for fiction that pressed in on me.

The first of these interruptions was, naturally enough, a novel about the death of a parent. The parent in this case, though, was an elderly mother. A difficult woman, a prima donna of sorts, who comes to stay with her middle-aged son for some months on her way to a retirement community. A woman who bore certain similarities to my own mother— though she didn't have an eighth of my mother's charm. Still, it amused me to think it was perhaps to appease the spirit of my mother, competitive and narcissistic as she was, that I had conjured this book. It made perfect sense in terms of the family dynamics, didn't it? I had to cope with her first. She *came* first. First, her book; then—only then—Dad's.

So I wrote *The Distinguished Guest*. And when I was done several years later, when it was off to the publisher, I turned back again to my father, to the memoir. As I had the first time, I hauled out the box of family papers; once again I hired an assistant to find out what the latest in Alzheimer's research was. And for the second time, after a period of working on it, I hit a kind of dead end—the magic of appeasement be damned.

I began to think my problem had to do with voice. With the fact that I was accustomed to using the first person only fictionally, hiding behind an imagined speaker who might be close to who I was but was not 'I.' *I* never had to own any of the thoughts and ideas and feelings I described in a novel; they belonged to my 'employees,' as Grace Paley once called her characters. Here, in the nonfiction work, I was self-employed, and I was having trouble figuring out how far forward I wanted to step, how much of the real 'I' to expose. At least that's what I told myself.

I thought it might be helpful to me to write a personal essay or two, to practice using a nonfictive first-person voice in some shorter works that would be less difficult for me emotionally than the book about my father's death. I began to take on a few journalism assignments, something I'd always turned away from before.

It did help. In the short essays I wrote, I could feel the breaking down of the scrim that had hung between me as first-person narrator and my imaginary reader. And even though the essays were not, in fact, themselves very intimate, I found myself writing comfortably and intimately in them.

But in the meantime, while I was working

on this problem of voice, along came another idea for a novel, a novel that rescued me again from the memoir, a novel called, appropriately enough, *While I Was Gone.* When I'd finished it, though, the memoir was still waiting, still prodding me.

I started again, with the more assured voice I'd taught myself in my essays. But as the *writing* began to come with greater ease, what I discovered was a more basic confusion on my part—the underlying question about why I was doing this, about what its truest, deepest aim was.

It made me think of the way I'd taught fiction when that was how I was making my living—of what I would have said to a student writer as confused as I still was about what I was writing. How I would start her thinking about what to do. *What drew you here?* I'd ask. What's making you want to record this? What's the point, for you? And how can you make that apparent? How can you *embody* that in what you put on the page?

I had often quoted Flannery O'Connor on writing to my students, in particular a passage from one of her beautiful essays in *Mystery and Manners.* In it she says:

St. Cyril of Jerusalem, in instructing catechumens, wrote: 'The dragon sits by the side of the road, watching those who pass. Beware lest he devour you. We go to the Father of Souls, but it is necessary to pass by the dragon.' No matter what form the dragon may take [she goes on], it is of this mysterious passage past him, or into his jaws, that stories of any depth will always be concerned to tell.

When I cited this passage with my students, I went on to secularize its meaning, something that would have horrified O'Connor, of course, but which was useful to me and, I think, to them. I spoke of the necessity for fiction to construct a *problem*, spiritual or no, for its characters, to ask them to solve it, and to watch them in their attempts: whether they triumph (slay the dragon); whether they're defeated (are slain, devoured); whether they win, but lose so much in the process that it's barely worth the prize; whether, as in some more modern work, we leave them at the moment they realize there *is* a dragon they're going to have to fight—or flee. In all these cases, I'd say to my students, the question for you as you start writing is, What is it that your character needs to struggle with? What's the right dragon for exactly the person you've created? What is the nature of the conflict, implicit or explicit, that you're asking the reader to witness and consider? It's understanding this about your own story, I'd argue to them, that makes it compelling to others.

And now I asked myself these same questions about the characters in the memoir.

For my father, the dragon was clear. It was his illness and what he would make of it, how he would deal with it. That part of the narrative was the easy part, in a certain sense.

But I was present in the memoir too. And I hadn't asked myself what my dragon was, what my character was struggling with in this story and its aftermath, what thing she'd vanquish or be vanquished by. I hadn't even accepted myself as a character in this sense up to then. Now I had to.

\*     \*     \*

For my father's memorial service in July, my sister had asked me to read Psalm 103, the one that begins, 'Bless the Lord, O my soul; and all that is within me, bless his holy name.' It speaks—with bitter irony, it had seemed to me as I prepared to read it at the service—of God's mercy:

> Who forgiveth all thine iniquities; who healeth all thy diseases; who redeemeth thy life from destruction; who satisfieth thy mouth with good things; so that thy youth is renewed like the eagle's.

It speaks of our inconsequence by comparison with God's goodness:

211

For he knoweth our frame; he remembereth that we are dust. As for man, his days are as grass; as a flower of the field, so he flourisheth. For the wind passeth over it, and it is gone; and the place thereof shall know it no more.

I stood in the little white wooden church in the clearing in New Hampshire and spoke these lines to my father's friends, his family: I, who had seen my father stop eating; who had, as long as I could, fed him water from a straw, drop by drop onto his parched tongue, while he was dying. Who watched him turn into a wizened tiny form in diapers in his bed, all beaky nose and clutching hands.

The memory of this was still fiercely alive in me when I began this memoir. And what I initially hoped it would do, the writing of it, was to assuage this horror and grief by insisting, I saw now, that my father was *not* as a flower of the field, dammit; there was sense, meaning, to be made of his life in terms of a narrative structure, an explanation of his self—the story of my father—as narrated by me.

The dragon for me was the disorder and oblivion that marked his dying and death. That's what I had been struggling with. That's what I'd seen myself as conquering as I wrote. I, the writer, would redeem my father, I would snatch him back from the meaninglessness of

Alzheimer's disease, from being as the flower in the field when the wind passes over it. *This* was my struggle, I thought. *This* was why I had undertaken the memoir in the first place. And at this point, for a while, this worked for me as a focus for the book.

And then it didn't. Another novel interrupted me, and by the time I returned yet again to the memoir and began what I was sure would be my last revision, I *literally* saw things differently too.

\*     \*     \*

I have some confidence by now in the unconscious processes of writing, those processes that bring me certain scenes, certain details, to work with. I believe it takes a fully conscious mind to do the work of writing, to bring things *around*, as it were; but I think there's often something deeply revelatory about the detail or the plot element that just 'occurs' to you out of the blue: the anecdote you overheard years earlier and remember now; the memory that wakes you in the night; the odd part of a story someone tells you that stays with you and seems to fit into what you're working on. These seem to me to be the very things worth examining and reexamining when you ask yourself those important questions about the deepest meaning of what you're writing.

I still had a number of such 'gifts' to try to make sense of, some of which came to me even after my father died, long after what I would have thought was the end of that possibility. In fact, the very processes of writing the memoir had called up many of these—memories, images, facts. Others arrived in unanticipated ways, like those letters about whether to resist conscription. It was when I began to go through my notes, through these *bits*, as I called them—things I'd put into my files to use, without knowing why—that I felt confused again about my own intentions.

For instance, I'd made a note of a story told me only a few weeks before my father died by Nancy, the woman I'd hired to take him for a walk each day. She'd been with him one afternoon, keeping up a semblance of normal human chatter as he made his way on his by-now very peculiar and compulsive circuit of the halls. They arrived finally at a lounge, Nancy trailing Dad. There was a group gathered inside, gathered with a leader. The group was singing. My dad stopped.

Ah! They were singing hymns.

He went into the room and Nancy followed. Hymnals had been distributed among the old women, and they were working their way through all the verses of song after song.

'And that old man,' Nancy said, 'he just threw his head back and sang along with them. Every verse. Every word. *He* didn't need any books.'

I thought about that, thought about the fact that I could usually calm Dad when he was agitated by singing hymns or reading the Bible. Something in those familiar words, those cadences, was consoling to him, even when he was lost in his terrors. I've described my pride, my relief, that my father always knew me. But it seemed to me now that even longer than he knew me, even more deeply than he knew me, he knew his faith—he remembered the words, the rituals connected with belief, and found comfort in them. How did this fit my notion of *my* redeeming him?

Another *bit* in my files was the copy of a short eulogy given at Princeton Theological Seminary by a colleague of my father's. The text sought to explain what was special about him—which was difficult, actually, for my father was a painstakingly thorough but not startlingly original scholar. He was a generous and attentive teacher, but not a dynamic or exciting one. He was a loyal, faithful, hardworking colleague, but not a charming or easygoing one. He was, I think, incapable of falsity, but his truthfulness was dispassionate, disinterested.

This memorial statement began:

On the wall of the office of the Academic Dean, when James H. Nichols was the incumbent, there hung a framed, cross-

215

stitched message which in a quiet way dominated the room. It seemed to set the tone. The text was from Calvin's *Institutes* and it read:

'We are not our own: let not our reason nor our will, therefore, sway our plans and deeds.

'We are not our own: let us therefore not set it as our goal to seek what is expedient for us according to the flesh.

'We are not our own: insofar as we can, let us therefore forget ourselves and all that is ours.

'Conversely, we are God's: let us therefore live for him and die for him.

'We are God's: let his wisdom and will therefore rule all our actions.

'We are God's: let all parts of our life accordingly strive toward him as our only lawful goal.'

This was important, I knew. I remembered that sampler, I remembered the words of Calvin. I knew these words were something I had to make use of in explaining my father. But how?

Then there was the story my father loved to tell about a colleague of his at the University of Chicago, where he taught for twenty-five years, a colleague named Charles Hartshorne, a theologian. The story is possibly apocryphal; I've heard similar ones about other academics.

216

It goes this way: One fine day, Hartshorne had gone for a walk, wheeling his infant daughter Emily in a carriage. He'd run into a colleague somewhere on campus and gotten into a passionate and intriguing discussion, which went on for quite a while. When he returned home, his wife asked, 'But Charles, where's the baby?'

Here my father's face would dramatize blankness, then a dawning horror. The baby! Charles Hartshorne had simply forgotten her when he got so involved. Involved, of course, in talking about *important* things—about God.

The story didn't end badly. In that more innocent time, they retrieved Emily without incident from wherever on campus her father had parked her and presumably lived happily ever after.

Of course, I understood my stake in this story. I was Emily, left in her carriage, forgotten when the excitement of the other part of his life claimed her father. It was a cautionary tale, then; but I couldn't quite see what it cautioned against, what useful lesson I might derive from it. For what control did we have over our fathers, Baby Emily and I? None. How could we make our lives more real, more pressing, to them? We couldn't.

What I knew, what I understood, was that the threat of Charles Hartshorne's kind of forgetting and the reality of that kind of distraction were a part of who my father was.

There was an impartiality, and therefore a distance, in even my father's closest and most loving attention. I don't know if he ever would have done exactly what Charles Hartshorne is supposed to have done, but I certainly knew him to be capable of forgetfulness of what to him seemed mundane or unimportant, and this occasionally included obligations he'd undertaken to one of us or to my mother. The anecdote seemed to me to reflect the nightmare side of living with someone whose first allegiance is elsewhere, is otherworldly. You are left, you are abandoned. You have no real importance in the great scheme of things.

Putting all this together as I worked on the memoir, what I had initially concluded was that his Alzheimer's disease in a sense merely exacerbated a lifelong feeling of loss I had about my father. *My father was not his own.* Therefore he couldn't be anyone else's—and he wasn't. He couldn't be my mother's, he couldn't be mine or my siblings'—though I acted out, I was *bad* in an attempt to make him claim me. He *did* notice that. He tried to help. Always he was gentle, dispassionate, understanding, disinterested, wise. An abstract father. A father who might forget you if what he was thinking about at the moment was more compelling to him.

This, I had thought, must be what gave Alzheimer's disease its peculiar emotional potency for me, even beyond the tremendous power it exerts in every family's life where someone suffers from it. It took my father away, yes. But it reminded me that my father had long since been taken. He'd been gone, claimed elsewhere—by his beliefs, by his convictions, by the way they dovetailed with whom he'd become, growing up with the peculiarly Victorian and religious upbringing he'd had.

Another of the memories I'd recorded but didn't know where to use in the memoir was of being, as a child, terrified by the passage in the gospel of Matthew in which Jesus speaks of a man's most serious spiritual foes as being in his own household: his intimates.

He that loveth father or mother more than me is not worthy of me: and he that loveth son or daughter more than me is not worthy of me. And he that taketh not his cross, and followeth after me, is not worthy of me. He that findeth his life shall lose it: and he that loseth his life for my sake shall find it.

But I *was* that daughter, that daughter to be discarded, lost with the rest of the believer's worldly life. This couldn't be right. My parents had to love me more than they loved Jesus! Wasn't that what parents were for? To love us best of all?

And now here in my middle age had come

Alzheimer's disease, terrifying me once more as my father left me behind once more. It seemed to me that this was my true struggle in writing my memoir—the revisiting of this childhood fear of abandonment, an abandonment you couldn't argue with or even confront without sounding infantile, unworthy. The dragon for me was the course of the disease itself—not because it took my father from me but because it took him from me *again.* And what I was confronting and dealing with as I wrote was that terror, that selfish childish terror.

This was what I had come to as I structured the final version of my Alzheimer's memoir, as I thought of it. As I pulled my material together for a last time.

\*　　　\*　　　\*

But of course what I felt as I actually did the writing was not despair or terror or loss at all. Was very much their opposite. Was pleasure. I *liked* it. I liked doing the research, finding out about the disease. I liked remembering my father, searching for the words to call him up, even to call him up in his illness. It comforted me. It excited me. I remember after a public reading of a portion of the memoir—the chapter that explains the way certain abilities are destroyed in the Alzheimer's patient's brain—a friend said to me that there had been a lively interest audible in my voice as I read, that my fascination with the material was evident.

Instantly I recognized the truth in what she said, and I felt guilty. I felt *caught in the act* somehow. I started to make excuses for myself.

She realized she'd made me uncomfortable. No, no, she said. What she'd meant was that the ability to take that kind of pleasure in my work, in what I was writing, was surely a gift my father had given me.

And as soon as she said it, I felt it: it *was* pleasure, writing, and it *did* connect me to him. It brought him back to me, even as I used it to describe his disappearance.

My father had been deeply involved in my writing life, maybe in part because he wished my mother might have had the opportunities and rewards I was having. In any case, it was during the years I was struggling to write and then having my first small successes that he and I were closest—the very years, of course, in which he began to be symptomatic. He was the one I called when my first story was taken, when *The Atlantic* accepted another story, when there was an offer on *The Good Mother*, my first published novel. His uncomplicated pride and his wonderful dry laugh of delight on the other end of the line were as gratifying to me as any other part of my pleasure in those events in my writing life.

And one of my markers of loss had occurred

when I took an early copy of my second novel out to Sutton Hill to give to him. I had dedicated it to him, and I meant that to be part of my gift. But it was too late. I hadn't finished it in time. He couldn't take in the dedication, and he misunderstood what I gave him; he saw it not as a book—in spite of the fancy jacket with my photo on the back—but as an unfinished project I was asking for his help with, as a student or colleague might have. He thanked me for it and said he wasn't sure when he would get around to going through it for me. And then he laughed and shook his head ruefully and said, 'I just don't seem to be able to get as much done as I used to.'

In the days and weeks following my father's death, many people wrote to me and to my brothers and sister about him, letters that called him up whole from various stages of his life. Wonderful loving letters that didn't begin to heal me until long afterward. I still have them. Selfishly, one of the most moving passages to me in all of them is this, from a dear friend of his:

> And did you know of one of our last meetings, when his illness had already begun, and he came to our house holding in his hand, like a precious, even sacred object, a review of *The Good Mother*, which he showed us with a shy pride?

No, I hadn't known that, though I'd taken pleasure in his pleasure in my success.

Even now, I often think of my father when I write. I think of the self-discipline I've inherited from him that drives me to my desk each day. Of the intellectual excitement I feel in doing the research I invariably have to do on a book. Of the sense I have as I work of being *in my element*, something he clearly felt too when he sat in his study day after day and looked up from his work at our lives passing by. It seems right, then, only natural, that I should have found even the writing of the details of his illness consoling.

Consoling, and also transformational. Because as I wrote, as I held up the bits and pieces I'd gathered to make the memoir from, I learned from them. I changed, and my understanding of things changed. I was revising once again.

I have spoken of my father's absence, of the revelation of my sense of loss of him, as a child, then as an adult, which came to me while I worked on this memoir. But what I didn't see until near the end of working on it was that he was present to me throughout its writing too. And partly as a result of that, certain incidents had gradually taken on a new meaning, a different meaning, as I wrote.

For instance, as I reworked the passage in the second chapter about the moment in which my father takes in the nature of what is going to happen to him and is, in a sense, *bemused* by it, I realized it contained a corrective to the sense of loss in the Charles Hartshorne story—the positive side to living with someone who *was not his own.* And in general, his acceptance of his illness—an illness that would take his intellect, his connection with other people, his ability to speak, to eat, to walk, to reason—seemed to speak of the inner resources he had because he was God's, as he saw it. He thought of this illness without ego, precisely *without* the sense of self and grief for the loss of self that would afflict me if I found I had Alzheimer's disease. In this way, the way in which I am very much 'my own' for better or worse, my father was not. This was the source for him of an almost unfathomable strength as he began his slow decline. And this was part, too, of who he was.

The colleague who wrote about the Calvin quote hanging in my father's office called him 'self-effacing to a fault.' I have called him self-effacing too, even in these pages. But as I have thought about him, as I've worked my way through all the material I assembled, I've realized that I don't think that's so. Self-effacement implies an action taken, a willed result—*he erased himself.*

My sense of my father has come to be that he simply didn't have that kind of *self* in the first place: the kind of post-Freudian, self-aware self most of us know all too well; the

224

kind of self-conscious self most of us haul with us through life; the kind of self tortured by self-analysis that my mother had; the kind of well-developed, well-scrutinized set of feelings and sensibilities that, I confess, I take pride in in myself.

The drama that brought me to this memoir was my father's illness and what it meant in my life. But there was another drama that occurred long after he died, that occurred as I was writing. The pieces I'd assembled, I discovered, made a different kind of story from the one I'd thought I was working on, and it wasn't at all the story of a *self*, narrated by me. No, what I came to see by accumulating my material, by holding it up and looking at it again and again, by revising and revising and revising over the years, was that there was no such narrative to be made of my father's life.

This is my final version, then, of the story. Most of the book is taken up with my father— it was what happened to him, after all, that caused me to grieve, and to struggle. And to learn. But *what* I learned was that in this way, as in so many other ways, my father didn't need me to rescue him, to make sense of his life. He accepted what was happening to him, the way he was fracturing and breaking apart, as he had accepted it in possibility well before it happened. For him his life and death already made sense. For him, Psalm 103 could be read through without irony to its conclusion, which goes as follows:

> But the mercy of the Lord is from
> everlasting to everlasting upon them that
> fear him, and his righteousness unto
> children's children; to such as keep his
> covenant, and to those that remember his
> commandments to do them . . . Bless the
> Lord, O my soul.

I don't remember if I read this psalm to
calm him when he was in one of his violent
panics; I might have. And it might have been
among the many psalms I read to comfort him
while he was dying, but I don't remember that
either; I hope it was. I think it might have
comforted him: just the familiar rhythms, the
old words, and the deep faith they describe.

My comfort is different, but, like his, it has
come from what is most central in my life. I've
called him up over and over and in a variety of
ways as I thought and wrote this memoir. And
he's come to me over and over, and more and
more clearly. I've *revised* him, as I've revised
my ideas about what I was doing, calling him
up. For it is by writing, by the simultaneously
pleasurable and painful processes of working
my way through the material I collected and
made over the years I labored on this memoir,
that I've come to see that his consolation
would always have lain beyond the reach of
any story I could have made of his life. But it is

by the making of the story, and by everything that changed in my understanding of him and of myself as I made it, that I have been, as the writer that I am, also consoled.

# ACKNOWLEDGMENTS

This is a book that I needed help to write, and I got it from a number of generous and skillful people. I'd like to thank them here. Judy Watkins dug up and annotated articles and films and books and whole magazines for me on Alzheimer's disease and the latest—and earliest—thinking about it. Maxine Groffsky and Doug Bauer read multiple early drafts and were critical and kind and helpful and patient. My editor, Jordan Pavlin, made a number of suggestions about my final draft which made the book more exactly what I'd wanted it to be. Aleister Saunders kindly read through the passages that deal most directly with the science of the illness and made several suggestions for more precise language. I'm enormously grateful to all of them.

Several books were important to me as I tried to understand the brain and memory and the nature of my father's illness. They are *The Engine of Reason, The Seat of the Soul: A Philosophical Journey into the Brain*, by Paul M. Churchland; *Searching for Memory: the Brain, the Mind, and the Past*, by Daniel L. Schacter; *Descartes' Error: Emotion, Reason, and the Human Brain*, by Antonio R. Damasio; *Memory's Ghost: The Strange Tale of Mr. M and the Nature of Memory*, by Philip J. Hilts;

and *The Forgetting: Alzheimer's: Portrait of an Epidemic*, by David Shenk.

Most of all I'm grateful to Doug Bauer and Ben Miller, who buoyed me through life while my father was ill and dying.

# A NOTE ABOUT THE AUTHOR

Sue Miller is the best-selling author of *The World Below While I Was Gone*, *The Distinguished Guest*, *For Love*, *Family Pictures*, *Inventing the Abbott*, and *The Good Mother*. She lives in Boston, Massachusetts.

# Chivers Large Print Direct

If you have enjoyed this Large Print book and would like to build up your own collection of Large Print books and have them delivered direct to your door, please contact **Chivers Large Print Direct**.

**Chivers Large Print Direct** offers you a full service:

✧ **Created to support your local library**

✧ **Delivery direct to your door**

✧ **Easy-to-read type and attractively bound**

✧ **The very best authors**

✧ **Special low prices**

For further details either call Customer Services on 01225 443400 or write to us at

**Chivers Large Print Direct**
**FREEPOST (BA 1686/1)**
**Bath**
**BA1 3QZ**